JAPAN ~ PORTRAIT OF PARADOX

JAPAN ~

Portrait of Paradox

QUENTIN CREWE

THOMAS NELSON & SONS

Edinburgh   NEW YORK   *Toronto*

First American Edition 1962

Originally published in Great Britain
under the title *A Curse of Blossom*

© *1960 by Quentin Crewe*

All rights reserved under International
and Pan-American Conventions. Published
in New York by Thomas Nelson and Sons.

DESIGN BY FRANK KARPELES

Library of Congress Catalog Card Number: 62-10369

PRINTED IN THE UNITED STATES OF AMERICA

CONTENTS

		PAGE
	Foreword	11
I	TOKYO	15
II	THE PROFESSORS	31
III	COUNTRYSIDE	43
IV	HOUSE-HUNTING	56
V	THE INN	69
VI	THE HOUSE	111
VII	THE SCHOOLTEACHERS	117
VIII	NOTES ON JOURNEYS	138
IX	FESTIVALS	184
X	THE ABBOT	203
XI	THE STUDENTS	228
XII	THE POLITICIANS	241
XIII	THE QUAYSIDE	256

LIST OF ILLUSTRATIONS

(*between pages 96-97*)

1. *Fumio San dances in the bar dressed as a woman*

2. *Moku Yanagawa, our interpreter*

3. *The Inland Sea*

4. *Peace Square in Hiroshima*

5. *Hot Spring Baths*

6. *The village of Obama*

7. *The folk museum at Kurashiki*

8. *Mount Unzen*

9. *The temple of Saidaiji*

10. *The crush of the festival*

11. *Many boys climb up into the rafters to escape the crush of the festival*

12. *Osho San, the abbot of Shinjuan temple*

13. *Shinjuan Temple, founded by Ikkyu*

14. *Every time we left the temple Obā San bowed deeply*

15. *The journey down the Hozu rapids*

16. *Ozaki, one of the students*

17. *Inoue, another student*

18. *Kuma, the village where the seminar was held*

ACKNOWLEDGEMENTS

I would like to thank Mrs. Kay West for her help in preparing the manuscript as well as for her patience and encouragement. I am also extremely grateful to Miss Elizabeth Jane Howard and Dr. Ivan Morris for reading the manuscript and giving invaluable advice.

Q. C.

Acknowledgements to Illustrations

The author and publishers are grateful to the Japan Travel Association for permission to reproduce Illustrations 3, 4, 5, 6, 7, 8 and 15. They also wish to thank the Mayor of Saidaiji and Mr. W. A. White for their kind permission to reproduce Illustrations 9, 10 and 11 and 12, 13 and 14.

FOREWORD

To say why I went to Japan seems, in retrospect, almost impossible. My wife and I decided practically at random that we would go somewhere—that we needed, at that precise point in our lives, some new, totally different experience. Given that we wanted to go somewhere, anywhere, it just seemed to happen that we chose Japan. We set off to find what we liked, and to spend a year absorbing an atmosphere as remote as we could imagine. It is a little hard now to recapture what we did imagine. Perhaps this is one of the reasons that I find it difficult to say why we went.

Mine was an innocent's vision of the Orient. I pictured it quite clearly. I saw towns which shone with paper lanterns, streets which tinkled with small dangling bells, and at corners I imagined quiet, sapient old men brimful of the secrets of life, answering one's questions with oracular wisdom. I knew that the women would be dressed in fine brocades and that they would be carried in sedan chairs down roads overhung with colored decorations. The lampposts would be objects of fanciful enchantment; the children would be spherical creatures of laughter. Life would be lived easily—almost at a dragging pace; materialism would be despised, and cruelty would be commonplace. Language I thought of as being an endless singsong of twanging incomprehensibility. And, somewhere in the back of my mind, there was even a secret hope of ostrich carts, like the ones in *Around the World in Eighty Days*.

When I consider all this, I don't find it at all surprising that my reasons for going have disappeared. Certainly I can now think of a thousand reasons why I should like to go back to Japan—but just as certainly they are not the ones for which I went.

JAPAN ~ PORTRAIT OF PARADOX

JAPAN

CHAPTER ONE

TOKYO

A HEAD, in the distance, rose huge blankets of solid cloud wallowing up to meet us as we gradually lost height. We humped down through the swirls of mist and broke through to see below us the coastline of Japan. At no great height, we flew inland and then turned south toward Tokyo. The earth below, even in the shade, was green with an almost tropical richness. Sudden compact hills and valleys gave the land the appearance of a bright alligator's back, rumpled and hard. As we sank lower, we just had time to pick out the gray blotches which were villages, then we were in the haze of Tokyo encroaching like a huge brown fungus on the country-side.

The capital sprawls over an area of 221 square miles. In a taxi we drove for longer than an hour through dingy, grimy, colorless streets. Traffic whirled and hooted. Streetcars clanked and ground down potholed, half-paved streets; bicycles rushed like possessed Valkyrie from every hidden turning. In the unexpected tumult we looked hopefully about.

Battered wooden houses lined the litter-strewn streets with a gray dusty wall. No building for many miles stood

15

higher than two stories, and what color there was came only from garish advertisements. Even the ideographic lettering had little charm, formalized for simplicity in signwriting. Incongruously, every so often outside a shop stood a bright silhouette figure of a Coldstream guardsman painted on plywood. The people in hordes swarmed recklessly across the roads without a glance. They wore inelegant Western clothes, ill-becoming to their stumpy height. Most young girls had on a cross between a school jumper and a sailor suit, and the boys, with their bullet heads shaved so that every scar and imperfection on their scalps stood out, wore black high-buttoned tunics, like Prussian students, and sometimes a severe round cap and a stunted peak.

Slowly we came to the center and the town became more like every other capital in the world, with new high square blocks, in dull imitation of Western architecture. The taxi driver had for some time been trying to address me in a wild and sputtering English.

"America or Ingurissu?" he asked at length.

"English," I said, relieved at understanding something.

"Roid-Joj, Deesreary, Peet," he said.

"Eh?"

"Roid-Joj, Deesreary, Peet."

He repeated this cryptic phrase for many minutes before I finally grasped his meaning.

"Churchill, Eden, Macmillan," I replied at last.

"That's right, all prime minister," he said with satisfaction.

"All Ingurissu gentleman," he continued happily. Then in a tone of inquiry, "You lib caraban, Rondon?"

We went over this four or five times before I could answer, "Yes, I live in London but not in a caravan."

"You must be very rich not lib in caraban," he assured me. "Most all Ingurissu lib in caraban. I seen moobie."

I was unable to disabuse him of this impression before we arrived. But in spite of my imagined riches he resolutely refused any tip. It was the first cheerful thing for us in Japan. Taximen are not tipped.

Tokyo is the largest city in the world, the noisiest, the most untidy, but at the same time perhaps one of the most vital. As you stand on the sidewalk in the center of town, faces stream past you at shoulder level—sad faces, not so yellow as you expected. Faces of which all the features seem to be concentrated in a narrow strip down the middle—the eyes with their hooded lids, the nose flat and broad, and above all the mouth—finely chiseled, with the most pronounced lips of any people. It is the mouth that one notices in a crowd, not so much for the teeth—although sometimes these seem to run wild like paper streamers in front of a fan—but rather for the incredible expressiveness and mobility. But the Japanese face has another quality—that of sadness. Except for the children, and sometimes for the women, the Japanese smile little. As they come past you, they seem all to be driving themselves on an urgent despairing errand.

✓ More than nine million people live in Tokyo. It is the industrial center of Japan, the seat of government, the home of the Emperor. And yet it is even less representative of the whole country than New York City is of America. It is the place which has taken most from the West, and in doing so it has lost nearly all charm, nearly all culture—indeed almost its nationality. But what it has taken amounts to the worst aspects of the Western civilization. It is a city bigger than London, but it has an utterly inadequate sanitation system. It has more bars than any other town in the world, but the population has the least resistance to alcohol. It has strip-tease shows of a womenfolk who are best seen dressed. It has lavish Western hotels, run by a people whose whole code of behavior has been dictated by a system of personal introductions. It has more houses than any other city, but few street names and no regular numbers. A whole culture has been imposed on the town and accepted wholesale without the trouble of an examination into what lay behind the culture in its original form.

In the daytime, during the first few days we were there, we spent our time wandering round acclimatizing ourselves to the newness of the Far East. In spite of an initial similarity in the center of Tokyo to any other capital city in the world, there was of course an unfamiliarity in everything we saw. It was only by comparison with our later experiences that we realized how untypical Tokyo was.

We were trying to decide at that time where we should live, what we most wanted to do. We would go from place to place seeking advice and battling with the bureaucratic resistance of the official tourist offices. It was my ambition to live in a small Japanese village and there study the ways of ordinary Japanese people, living as nearly as possible in the traditional style of the country. It was difficult and exasperating, trying to get accurate, useful information. I remember Mr. Yamamoto of the Japanese Tourist Bureau, with whom

I spent several hours on three successive mornings poring over maps of Japan.

"What happens here?" I would ask, pointing to some blanker-looking space.

"Ah," he would say, "Niigata Prefecture—very remote. Quite impossible for you to live there."

He would then, as did all our advisers, recommend some tourist resort for which he would have quantities of leaflets, printed in rather whimsical English. I would then point to Nagano Prefecture.

"That might be rather nice—close to your Alps." I mentioned this because I had heard of a pleasant hotel in this area. I thought we might go there and look around for a house, using the hotel as a base.

"Couldn't we say in Shiojiri?"

"There is no hotel there."

"But there is," I said. "It is called the Nanten."

Mr. Yamamoto consulted a little list and had to agree that the Nanten did exist.

"Well, try and book us rooms there for tomorrow night, and we'll start looking from there."

Mr. Yamamoto disappeared, affecting to put in a telephone call. With irritating realism, he did not reappear for half an hour. When at last he came back, he bowed two or three times.

"Very sorry—no rooms at that hotel."

Later on I would have known better and made the telephone call myself.

Mr. Yamamoto's other great worry was to place me. He could not imagine what I was doing in Japan. At each new interview he would ask me innocently, "Ah, Mr. Crewe—you forgot to tell me yesterday who you are with."

"But I did tell you—I am with my wife and child."

"No—with whom you are associated. Your university?"

"I am not with any university."

"Well, then, your company? Or perhaps you are with the Asia Foundation? Or Rockefeller, or Ford? Or the British Council?"

It was an agony for Mr. Yamamoto that I was with no one. It was a matter of agitation to almost everyone I met in the course of a year's stay. They could not believe that one would travel—indeed almost exist—unless one were attached to some institution. It was not merely a question of money. They would have expected even a millionaire to be traveling under somebody's aegis. It was perhaps symptomatic of a fundamental difference between our two civilizations. For the Japanese the individual has, even today, less significance than for any Western nation. A man only acquires stature by virtue of the organization to which he belongs, and his position in it. They are a people of the community, believers in communal responsibility. This is a relic of the compact village life which lasted until very recent times, an agricultural system evolved partly because of the intractable nature of the countryside. Each village was likely to be sealed off in its own little valley, and was separated from the next by a journey of possibly several hours. Until shortly before the war, communal responsibility was a part of the law of the whole country. In allotted groups of five, each man was responsible for the good behavior of the other four. If one were to commit a crime the other four could be punished.

Moreover, the disgrace of any malefactor's action, apart from the legal aspects, fell on the whole of his village. While this is no longer strictly true, any man doing wrong would be acutely conscious of the shame it might bring upon his family or friends.

This theme of the unimportance of the individual occurs again and again; whereas in the case of collective responsibility it may work on the side of law and order, we shall see it working against enterprise, against freedom, against happiness—and, at its worst, in the form of its natural corollary, collective irresponsibility.

As we sought advice, going about from place to place, we slowly absorbed some of the atmosphere of the strange city. Behind the façade of Western buildings in the central, fashionable part of the town, lay a maze of little streets which seemed to be almost untouched by the general passion for everything Western. These little streets had no sidewalks. Pedestrians took priority over motor cars, straying haphazardly across the road as if the combustion engine had never been invented. There is all over Japan an almost lunatic unconcern about crossing the streets, about turning a corner on a bicycle, about driving a car. The Japanese seem so absorbed in whatever they are doing that no training or fear seems able to distract them. The streetcar stops are placed in the middle of the road, and if there is one waiting to leave it does not seem to occur to them that there could be anything between them and their intention of catching it.

The sides of the small streets are lined with shops, with their wares spilling and spreading out on to the roadside. The streets are full of people pushing and shoving, thronging busily along, pausing every so often to finger the goods on display. They seem mostly to do this only in shops where they are known. It seems that they deal almost entirely with acquaintances, except when they go to one of the large department stores. The result is that every transaction is accomplished by a nervous titter of polite conversation, inquiries after the health of the families of both parties, and endless bowing and sharp intakes of breath. Once one is involved in a conversation the world around is forgotten and all energy is devoted to the proper exchange of courtesies. It is nothing to see two women blocking a narrow alleyway for several minutes as they seesaw up and down in six or seven farewell bows.

The smells of these streets were at first almost overpowering, but at length one becomes accustomed to them and instinctively identifies the causes of them. In one place they are preparing the rice paste for the New Year Festival. In another it is the bean curd for breakfast soup. On Wednesdays it is the day for carting away the night soil.

In these streets the houses are wooden. Each one is built irregularly, jutting out or set back from its neighbor, higher or lower as the case may be. Most of them have windows of paper, some have glass, each has its sliding door, either on the street or a few paces down the passage beside the house. Everywhere are signs—huge boards of all colors covered in ideograms, scattered all over the buildings like a fallen shower of cards. In among them are concessions to the foreigner—advertisements for Coca-Cola, Lucky Strike or beefsteak. In these back streets live the ordinary people of Tokyo, struggling to keep their own heritage in conflict with

the huge office blocks and vast department stores which are
the new-found face of Tokyo. Linking them too with the
past is the huge Imperial Palace, secluded and forbidden, set
right in the middle of the business part of the city. Japan is
the only place where the ruler could still maintain, in such
a cramped capital, an area as large as London's Hyde Park
for his own private dwelling place.

Tokyo is a pleasant place to walk in. As a foreigner one is,
in the humbler streets, still stared at—but seldom, if ever,
is one bothered or importuned and there are virtually no
beggars. There is incident and life; a child may give way
to a wild tantrum which everyone stops to observe, a band
of Shinto priests and youths may go past in procession,
dressed in incongruous robes, and very occasionally you may
see a trotting man drawing a closed rickshaw, inside which
you can glimpse briefly a geisha. There are amusement parks
where a fair-ground atmosphere thrives next door to a Buddhist temple.

But it is by night that Tokyo takes on its full, strange, confused character. The people, who by day seem so engrossed
in their business, devote at night an almost demonic energy
to enjoying themselves. Nowhere else can offer so many
varied and curious ways of distracting its inhabitants—most
of them predictable and notable only for their being so much
more exaggerated than their equivalents elsewhere. There
are as many as thirty thousand bars, varying from enormous
palaces, with names like The Eden and Harem, to tiny ones,
with room enough only for two customers and with names
such as The Bar Lonely. In all these, from the biggest to the
smallest, from the most respectable to the least, there is a

flurry of girls waiting to look after you. Each bar tries to outdo the others with some gimmick to distinguish it. On the coldest nights, you may step out of the snow into a hot smoky room and find yourself embraced by girls in bathing suits. In another place all the girls will wear tailcoats. In one to which I went the hostesses wore black bathing suits, the lower half of which was made of a specially treated substance, so that you could strike a match on the girls' behinds as they passed by your table.

The Otowa was a small bar about a mile from the Imperial Palace. I went there for the first time with an introduction from a friend, having no idea what I should find. "It is a *kabuki* bar," my friend had said. At the door I was greeted by three romantic figures in full *kabuki* theatrical dress. We bowed and hissed agreeably on the doorstep, and they led me into the bar. It was pleasant and clean, the long counter running down the left, about five tables on the opposite side and, at the far end, a low stage covered with rush matting. I was the only visitor, and the three who had greeted me were joined by two others, also dressed in long colorful women's kimonos and elaborate piled-up wigs which seemed to be made of spun coal. The bar was dark and it was ten minutes before I realized that these exotic figures were all men.

Homosexuality in Japan is not regarded as anything disgraceful. In *The Chrysanthemum and the Sword,* Ruth Benedict says that it is accepted as a normal part of the circle of human relationships. She goes on to point out that the Japanese man would never involve himself in a homosexual relationship with another man of his own age. Rather he would find a youth. One of the students, whom I later got to know in Kyoto, told me that he would not be shocked to hear that a man was living with a young boy of fourteen, but that he might find it distasteful to think of two adults having such a relationship. In spite of the contortions, which the Japanese will go through to save face, they have little disapproval of private action. They do not mind if you get drunk, for they feel that a man has his own reasons for drunkenness, and a freedom in his private relationships.

There was nothing prurient about the Otowa bar. I was expected to accept their attitudes in the same way that they were prepared to accept mine. I spent the evening talking for preference to the young waiter, Toshio Oki. He was nineteen and came from a small village just south of Mount Fuji. Unlike the others, he was dressed in a simple man's kimono. His face had the soft pliancy of childhood, becoming pathetically eager and proud to have pleased me. He told me about his family, who earned a bare living from less than an acre of land. "I have left them," he said, "because there is not room for more than one son. I must make my own way."

The painted transvestist actors were teasing him about his struggles to talk English. I asked him what they were saying. "They are telling our happiness story," he said. "Of how you will take care of me and take me back to your country and I shall look after you. You will be my father."

It was my first experience of the wild need of Japanese youth for love and affection—a need to attach and subject themselves to an imagined figure, half master, half parent. It runs through the whole mass of the young people. The freedom with which they are brought up as children is abruptly ended with ruthless certainty at the age of puberty. Thereafter, the demands of duty replace the fondness of the family. The girls must learn to be obedient wives, the boys to be heads of households.

Toshio was not the only one in that bar who gave me a foretaste of the strains and stresses to which the Japanese seem almost eagerly to subject themselves. The Otowa belonged to a rich businessman, a nebulous figure in the background who had given the running of it to Fumio San. Fumio was a disappointed *kabuki* actor, as were all the men dressed up in the theatrical clothes, but he himself wore an ordinary kimono, like Toshio. There was a distinctive quality about him, one which made me wonder why he had not been more successful on the stage, for he had the moving, tapered face familiar from the eighteenth-century woodcuts of actors. He was effeminate, but his traditional long smooth features gave him a thoroughbred appearance—formal and stylized. When the others got up to dance one of the *kabuki* dances he came and sat beside me.

"Are you English?" he asked me.

I agreed that I was. I told him too that I was a writer.

"In England," he asked, "are writers good or bad men?"

"Good and bad, like everybody else."

"Mr. Spender, he is a good man, is he not?"

"Yes," I said, puzzled by these questions.

"But not all writers are good men like him?"

"No."

"Do most English writers hate the Japanese?"

"Why do you ask?"

It seemed that a few nights before, an English writer had

come into the bar, perhaps not knowing what sort of bar it
was. After a time he had become exasperated by the atmosphere of the place, and in protest had thrown a glass of
whisky in Fumio San's face. The result had surprised the
Englishman. Fumio San had done nothing. He hadn't hit out;
he hadn't replied. He had merely ignored the incident, and
the Englishman had left. Fumio asked me if I knew the
writer in question. As it happened, I did, and had heard
something of the incident. The writer had been irritated by
a girl in his party who was plainly attracted to Fumio and
by what he judged to be Fumio's smug complacency.

"But why did he do it?" Fumio asked me. "Was it because
I am Japanese?"

There seemed to me in these words to be a heart-rending
self-abasement—almost a denial of personality. Fumio was
a curious blend of personal vanity and national humility.
He had believed that the English writer was incensed not
at anything he had done but rather at the whole Japanese
race. Two nights after the episode he took a large overdose
of sleeping pills. He did not die. Perhaps it was merely a
theatrical gesture—a protest of a failed actor. Nevertheless
he did it, and was saved only after uncomfortable hours in
the hospital. There was much in this story that would later
become clear to me. The bland refusal of all Japanese men
to believe that they can be wrong, and the pathetic lack of
conviction in their country since defeat—the curious lack of
pugnacity even in the face of an insult. And above all the
nonchalant ease with which they rush into suicide.

The whole question of suicide is so inextricably bound up
with the character of the Japanese, their history, their codes

of honor—that it is hard to reach any conclusion about it without knowing from the inside everything which motivates the people of this country. It is not enough to pick on one aspect of their attitude in order to find an explanation for the fact that they have the highest suicide rate in the world, that nearly twenty-five thousand people kill themselves each year. It is not merely that they hold life to be less important than we do, nor that half the stories in the history books and three-quarters of the stories in their national theater extol suicide as an admirable feat, nor that they believe loss of face is an unbearable ignominy. It is rather all these things, coupled with an inborn love of despair and a deeply marked pride in sorrow.

The reasons given by people for committing suicide seem to us almost risible. A maid will hang herself because she has lost the money which her master gave her to do the shopping with. A boy will cut his throat because his mother has taken a lover. A carpenter will jump from a cliff because he has lost his chisel. A boy of eighteen will poison himself because he repents of having seduced his friend's sister. Even among the young people to whom I talked about this subject, those who had been brought up since the introduction of foreign education and foreign values, could still not quite get rid of the idea that there was something admirable about suicide. "I know it is shocking," a very young student said to me, "but I cannot forget the heroes of our history—the forty-seven ronin, for instance, who waited for three years to avenge their master and were then proud to die by their own hand— any more than you can resist a certain pride in the Battle of Trafalgar, even though you believe war to be wrong."

They do have a pride in the romance of *hara-kiri* and, even now that they have for the most part abandoned this particularly gruesome method of self-inflicted death, they manage to surround the gloomy facts with a certain aura of ritual. There are two fashionable places to kill oneself. People will travel five hundred miles to leap to their death in the correct surroundings. There is almost official acknowledgment of these two gory centers. The first is at Atami, particularly popular for double suicides, where there is a convenient cliff from which you may drop into the sea. At the end of a well-worn path to the promontory, there is a little notice: *Chotto matte, mo ichido kagaete miyo* (Wait a moment, please think once more). No injunction, one notices, not to do it if your mind is made up. No fence, no interference with private affairs.

The other favored place for suicide is a waterfall at Nikko, where a friend told me he saw the forsaken body of a boy which no one had bothered to remove. Nikko is a comparatively recent Mecca for suicides. Every schoolboy knows the words of the first youth who leaped to his death in this tourist beauty spot. His name was Misao Fujirama, a student of Tokyo First High School, who wrote a careful message which was found on his body after he jumped:

"How long is Time? How spacious are heaven and earth? I am going to measure their greatness with my body five feet tall. What authority does the philosopher Horatio have? I have always thought about these things, and after experiencing many mental agonies I have now decided to kill myself. I have no fear in my heart as I stand at the top of the waterfall. On the contrary, I now realize that great sorrow and great happiness can be the same."

There is the whole of it. Great sorrow is great happiness. It is almost a tenet of Japanese belief. One poem runs: *Ku wa raku no tane*—pain is the seed of happiness. This is reflected in almost every aspect of their lives. Their poetry is infused with the beauties of brief moments of sadness. They are attracted less by the green shoots of spring than by the falling autumn leaf. They love not the bright innocence of girlhood, but rather the lost moment of youth. They do not resist the moment when you have to buy chrysanthemums. Instead it is their imperial flower.

CHAPTER TWO

THE PROFESSORS

THE Tokaido Highway is to the Japanese a symbol of their history. This road which straggles from the old capital to the new, from Kyoto to Tokyo, serves a richer purpose for a Japanese even than Canterbury for an Englishman. It is a road unlike any other in the world. Not merely martial and triumphal as the Appian Way, not alone religious as the Pilgrim's Way, not just commercial as the Alaska Highway, but all of these and then more. It is a road of hate and love, of war and peace. A highway of riches and poverty, of religion and banditry.

So, then, if you tell a Japanese that you are to take this road, it can never seem to him a wholly commonplace undertaking. History, of which all the natives of this country are perpetually aware, rushes up at him and he makes a deep Japanese noise, impossible to reproduce, and breathes the word back at you. "*Aaah, Tokaido, Ah* soo-ooh *des'ka?*" It is the word itself which produces this effect. Just say, "I'm driving to Tokyo tomorrow," and he will accept the fact lightly.

It happened that I used the word Tokaido to a new friend,

31

Professor Nishiwaki. The professor, a sad, gray thinning man, was head of the English faculty of Keio University, and is a poet both in English and Japanese. "I am the T. S. Eliot of Japan, so they say—extraordinary thing," he told me at our first meeting. Nishiwaki always punctuates his conversation with the phrase "extraordinary thing," even when referring to the most usual occurrences. Indeed the whole of his spoken English seems bizarre until he reveals that at Oxford in the twenties he read Beowulf. Moreover, it is delivered in a jerky, inconsequential manner which characterizes even his Japanese. He is a kindly man and I was the cause of some agitation to him. He was bound to me, complicatedly, by the involved code of obligation which governs and colors all intercourse in Japan. I had asked him to help me choose some remote country village in which I could live. Restrained by courtesy he could not, baldly and usefully, tell me that he thought me mad to undertake such a thing, with no knowledge of Japanese and none of customs.

We sat, his family and mine, fencing this problem. I would inquire about some distant area.

"Ah, yes, very beautiful, but what about the Izu peninsula?" he would say naming, as Mr. Yamamoto had done, a popular resort. I would politely decline and suggest some other more forsaken place. The crisis came when his son, a boy of about sixteen, said that such and such a district might be dangerous.

"Dangerous? You mean we might be attacked?"

The father gave his son a savage silencing look.

"No, no, extraordinary thing, dangerous it might hap for

your baby, that is his meaning," Nishiwaki said adroitly. "No correct food, no hospital, extraordinary thing."

To save the situation I said we were thinking of driving down the Tokaido to Kyoto before deciding. We might even stay there a while.

"Aaah, Tokaido, Aaah soo-ooh *des'ka?"*

Life returned to normal. "You have taken from me a great burden from here," Nishiwaki announced, pressing the left side of his chest with both hands spread open wide. "Now you must meet my colleague, Professor Nishioka, he is an expert on the Tokaido."

The next night the two professors came to pick us up at our hotel and we traveled by taxi to Professor Nishioka's house. Nishiwaki is something of a card and, as we bumped along the glittering streets, he told us about Nishioka, who sat beside us.

"He lives in a garden city. Oho! The first garden city in Tokyo. And there he lives in splendor. Oho! A garden city 'straordinary thing. And what does he do in this garden city? Cultural geography. And in Japanese the word for cultural geography is very like the word for aeronautics. So when he was called up, they misheard what he said so they placed him in the Air Force. Very funny, tell them about it," he said to Nishioka.

There wasn't much to tell as he himself had told it all, so Nishiwaki went on.

"And he calculates. He has calculated that the world gets hotter and hotter for three hundred and seventy-five years, then gets colder again. Every seven hundred and fifty years it is at its hottest. It is getting hotter now, oho, 'straordinary thing. He has written a book on phallic symbols in Japan."

The last comment didn't apparently rate as extraordinary and Nishiwaki subsided into one of the quiet periods which always followed a stretch of conversation.

Nishioka, who had grunted in a noncommittal fashion throughout the description of himself was now occupied in directing the driver through the maze of the "garden city." Martha and I sat silently rehearsing all the instructions we had read and been told for behavior when visiting a Japanese house. Martha was holding the inevitable large box, usually of sticky cakes, which all guests must bring to their hosts. I struggled to memorize the long-drawn-out phrases of greeting and self-deprecation that accompany the equally protracted bowing which an encounter demands.

The taxi arrived outside a small house set back about twenty yards from the road. It was difficult in the darkness to judge its character. Dogs barked furiously and a maid came down the short path to greet us. It was only just in time that I prevented Martha from thrusting the cakes into her hand.

Struggling through an undulating mass of dogs, we came into the outer hall of the house, which was paved with smooth concrete and looked something like a small conservatory. The floor was damp with water, and on one side stood a large fish tank; plants were everywhere and birds of all sorts squeaked from a dozen cages hung around the walls. In one corner an alarmed badger peered out from a wooden box. We mounted the steep wide step at the farther end, shaking off our shoes as we did so, and placing our stock-

inged feet into one pair of the long row of slippers neatly
ranged along the top. Waiting for us stood Nishioka's wife,
a small young-looking woman dressed in a blue kimono with
a large yellow sash, called an *obi*, elaborately tied at the back
to form a stiff rectangle nearly one foot across.

Martha bowed and handed her the parcel. I bowed and
mumbled my phrases. It all seemed simpler than we had
expected. We went up a short, tiled ramp into the sitting
room. Mrs. Nishioka's mother and father were introduced
to us. Again we bowed and mumbled. But this time it was
not so easy because her parents, who were from the country,
were not so accustomed to the haphazard ways of foreigners.
We straightened up, thinking we had once again acquitted
ourselves adequately and looked around the room. Then we
suddenly noticed that the two old people had once more
sunk their heads to their knees. Hurriedly we did the same.
They started up, then seeing us still down they bowed again.
So for five more bows we seesawed, until at last we rose at
the same moment.

The room, which finally we could look at, was a disappointment. Professor Nishioka had, for the most part, abandoned
all tradition in his furnishing. Instead of the bare mat floors
and walls we had expected, there were carpets and a clutter
of bookshelves, bird cages and fish tanks. A large kitchen
table stood near the stove and sink over which, suspended
on a bracket, was a television set. Forming three sides of a
square around a low table were a large sofa and six arm-
chairs crushed together and covered with a tartan material.

Mrs. Nishioka brought earthenware cups of green tea and,
on small plates, a gray cake wrapped in a bay leaf, one for

each of us. Japanese cakes are sweet and glutinous, compounded of sugar and bean paste.

"They will be too sweet for you."

"Oh, no, they will be delicious."

"Our cakes are no good. I am sorry."

"No, they look excellent. We are looking forward to them."

"I am sorry. Do not touch them. Our cakes are revolting."

There was nothing to be done but eat them.

"You must see," the professor told us, "the scrapbook of my visit to America."

Several large albums were produced and we turned the leaves. First came a photograph of the professor standing by the door of his house saying good-by, a photograph of his luggage, then several of his family waving. The airport was treated with equal thoroughness. The next page was entirely devoted to the cover and stub of his ticket and some baggage labels. The following one had the menu of dinner on the airplane, the paper napkin he had used and the tops of the cardboard pots of salt and cream. So we followed his journey through photographs, match boxes, laundry slips and bills for hamburgers, notes and hat checks until, on the final page, came a letter from the airline apologizing for some delay in his flight home because of engine trouble. We were later to get used to the Japanese passion for detail.

We told Nishioka of our proposal to drive down the Tokaido. He himself had walked the whole length of it once, and bicycled and driven down it many times. On these journeys he had taken innumerable photographs. With these and from other old photographs, drawings and etchings he has built up a collection of slides, covering every aspect of the highway. Using as a basis the wood-block prints executed in 1834 by Hiroshige, of the fifty-three stations on the Tokaido, he has documented the recent history of the road with a thoroughness as exhaustive as the scrapbooks of his own journey.

For two hours he showed us the slides and in that time we covered but nine of the fifty-three stages. Yet, in those few stages, he presented a picture of the changes in Japan during one hundred years that it would otherwise be impossible to guess at, and one which gave a perspective no book could achieve.

The first nine stages were the ones we were to drive by car the next day—the road from the center of Tokyo to Hakone, a village from which we should first see Mount Fuji. The distance is roughly fifty miles. Today the way lies through the most heavily industrialized country in Japan. Ninety years ago it was all arable.

The pictures Nishioka shone on to his screen might have been an object lesson devised by the National Trust. Each group of slides started with the simple economical lines of a woodcut by Hiroshige. The artistic merit of Hiroshige is not great. His works are unoriginally faithful to the Japanese tradition and his colors are obvious and hardly suffer when, as often happens, they are changed in the mass of reproductions made for post cards, leaflets and match-box covers. On the other hand, within his limits, he produced some of the most accurate interpretations of the Japanese landscape. If they were true of his time, then they were true also of the preceding three hundred years, for during those three centuries Japan had been deliberately restrained from change.

Hiroshige's pictures show a land of agriculture, of men walking and of rulers riding, a countryside of pretty bridges and of rice fields. There are in his world no vehicles, no chimneys, no ships which could go more than a few furlongs from the shore. There are swords but no gunpowder, wooden houses but no brick, poetry but no printing works. There is fighting but no war. It is a closed-in, self-sufficient land.

After each Hiroshige woodcut came slides of the same scenes as they gradually developed. The paddies gave way first to houses, then to factories. Curved wooden bridges yielded to stone ones and finally to iron girders. Costume lost its embellishment and then its form. Ginza, the main street of Tokyo, took on for a while the air of a Regency English country town, with balconies and pillars; swept these aside in favor of a 1920's suburban main street; and at last rose up with twelve-story concrete masses. Rocky shores became a maze of piers and whole villages were swallowed and lost their identity in the passage of only a year or two. The shrines and monuments alone remained, enveloped by a welter of incongruous buildings. Carriages came and went again, superseded by the car. Poetry was dimmed, thrust aside by signs, hoardings and glaring neon. The china cat with one arm raised in welcome outside inns was replaced by a plain notice: "Approved by the Japanese Tourist Bureau." Men swinging from a gibbet, servants of a revolutionary lord, had their sequel in an Engishman assassinated for crossing the path of a dignitary and, perhaps, in the giant ammunition plants. The first two of these caused a burst of laughter among the professors' families.

It was an obvious story, surprising only in its suddenness.

The same could be told of England or America. Yet there seemed a difference. Here was a complete, if stunted, culture. It was insecure certainly, but in its way it was developed. Then came the change, not as in England or America a natural growth, but here by the violent addition of another culture, partly imposed and partly snatched at with a rapacious avidity, an exaggerated greed for all things new. Japanese culture was decaying, yet it had an innate beauty. This beauty was the first casualty under the impact, not of Western philosophy, but of Western materials taken wholesale without their context.

In one set of slides we followed the fate of an enchanting bridge. When first we saw it, it was an elegant narrow stone bridge raised in a perfect arc above a gentle river. Soon another wide bare bridge was built in a more convenient, less apt, place two hundred yards downstream. Around the new bridge houses clustered rapidly. They spread until they obscured the lines of the disused bridge. The last picture showed only the crumbled pillars at the water's edge now supporting the corner of a murky shop, and in the middle of the river a forlorn mass of rubble crowned with one brief remnant of curved stone.

"It's too sad," I said.

"Too sad?" the professors laughed. "Oh, maybe a little, but too sad? Not too sad." They laughed some more.

It is a strength and a weakness, this disregard for change. It is a comfortable feeling not to care too deeply for something which is lost, moreover the Japanese are used to destruction. Their most venerated temples have so often been destroyed by fire. They rebuild them exactly as they were, and are, in a way no Westerner could be, just as satisfied with the new article as they were with the old. Indeed, their most sacred Shinto temple at Ise is torn down and rebuilt on precisely the same pattern every twenty years. But this power of resignation carries with it the feeble beliefs that success is justice, that the vanquished is necessarily wrong, that the fittest not only survives but in surviving becomes morally superior.

Professor Nishioka himself provides an example of this unquestioning surrender to triumph and success. The slides over, we sat round the table drinking this time black tea, generously laced with Scotch whisky. Nishioka told us now a bit more about his experiences in the Air Force. He acquired a certain proficiency in his unexpected duties but was eventually taken prisoner in Burma.

"How were you treated?" I asked.

"Oh, very well," he said. "I became an interpreter at Mountbatten's headquarters."

I gazed at him blankly. I tried to visualize what my reaction would have been to a similar announcement from an Englishman that he had, when captured, willingly served on Rommel's staff.

"He had a good time, 'straordinary thing," Nishiwaki beamed absently.

Nishioka was not regarded as a traitor, he had merely behaved sensibly. He had recognized in his defeat the superiority of his conquerors. So it was with nearly all Japanese prisoners of war. Capture was a disgrace, it placed them in a moral vacuum. If they did not commit suicide, and progressively fewer did as the war continued, they surrendered not

only their persons but also their allegiance. They revealed to
interrogators all that they knew of their country's secrets.
They drew maps of defenses, they gave away facts and
figures without much thought for their compatriots' fate.
The plainer it became that Japan would lose the war the
more readily they helped the enemy's cause. They embraced
the victors, for victory proved them right.

The Western peoples want to win wars because they believe they are fighting for some inviolable truth. If they lose,
they do not rest until they can rise again for their cause.
They often mistake what is right, but they will always cloak
infamy in the paraphernalia of justice, for without God on
their side, they cannot fight. The Japanese want to win wars
for their gods—keeping on the side of the gods. If they win
they are right. If they lose they are wrong.

For the Americans and English this characteristic was as
valuable as it was incomprehensible. It made it possible for
them to impose on the Japanese foreign morals and beliefs
and new forms of government. The Japanese accepted them,
as far as they understood them, humbly and contentedly.
Japanese history shows that, despite the fact that at present
she is still weighed down by tradition, she will, for the sake
of expediency, abandon it.

In the fifth century Japan adopted Chinese culture, Chinese
writing, Chinese architecture. Chinese religion and Chinese
methods of government were also imported. They were
adjusted to suit Japanese needs. The writing was modified.
The architecture was softened to agree with the less exaggerated Japanese taste. The religion cast off the depths
of philosophy foreign to Japanese nature and, by incredible

contortions of both Buddhism and Shinto, was made compatible with the native beliefs. The methods of government were similarly adapted. Japan was enabled, by borrowing a way of life, to establish herself firmly and to survive independently until the middle of the nineteenth century.

Fear of colonization brought about the next great change. Japan was an open target for British, French or American imperialism. She could no longer hide from the world. Under the Emperor Meiji in 1868 she reached out once again for whatever other civilization had to offer. Arms, industry and a government established on a copy of the Prussian constitution saved Japan's independence. They brought too a wild ambition.

Tried out, the ambition failed. It was wrong. They had taken the wrong bits of Western culture. The situation dictated that they should take the right bits. So they did—in some degree.

But what was sensible in 1945 may not always be so. Japan is Asian. Where Asia will go she, in her expedient heart, believes she must go—even lead. America has retired. Japan's happy acceptance has made her once more independent. Japan may, in the abstract, dislike communism. She may denounce it freely. At the same time, Japan wants to trade with Asia. She wants to maintain her independence. In the face of danger she does not count the cost of change. She accepts and adapts.

CHAPTER THREE

COUNTRYSIDE

W<small>E LEFT</small> Tokyo the next morning in a taxi. We were anxious to get away from the noise and the turmoil and to find, as soon as possible, somewhere to live. I had bought a baleful-looking, tired Chevrolet with a clutch pedal that went in and out on its own at a whim. The garage man from whom I got it had that affable, convincing unreliability of motor dealers, which transcends nationality. He had promised to deliver it in time for our departure, but the usual mysterious obstacles prevented him from doing so. He came to see us off and undertook to drive the car to Hakone himself in a day or so.

The driver of the hired car was nervous, fearful of scratching his huge American car. We crept rockingly through the suburbs of Tokyo over pitted roads. Tokyo merged with no interruption into Yokohama. Gray walls of streets all alike, all shabby and depressing. Then a toll road, away from the sea, closed in, not admitting the countryside, and soon Fujisawa City and again gray walls. Here we turned off, for a diversion back toward the coast of about an hour, to the Great Buddha at Kamakura. The muddy road led into the

43

north of this town. The driver stopped and pointed to a sludgy vacant lot.

"Park there?" he asked.

"No, somewhere drier."

We drove on. The town's narrow streets were choked with buses and coaches. The car eased slowly through. For twenty minutes we drove until we emerged on the other side of the town and started along the coast.

"Where is the Buddha?"

"We passed it. Where you said you didn't want to stop."

"But why do you think we came an hour out of our way? Why didn't you say the Buddha was there—we could see nothing."

He shrugged. "Foreigners are like that. I thought you didn't care. It was wet."

Indifferent, he drove back to the sludgy car park. Feeling foolish I bought him some fruit to eat while we went to look at the shrine. He thanked me but put it away without touching it, stolidly not caring, refusing plainly to condemn or to unbend. He was unaffected by anything to do with foreigners.

We had not seen the high gateway, for it was concealed by a cluster of dark trees. A stone path led through this screening wood and, passing the gate, came into the open. We had driven through flat country, but now green, sharp, wooded hills, rose unexpectedly where before we could not see them, hidden as they were by buildings and trees. In the foreground sat the massive Buddha. Unframed, unhoused, it sits. The hills like downs but more violent, chunkier, younger; the height of downs but not smoothed and soothing, rather roughly round like tumors—sudden perverse hills, shoot upward as a background. Before them, smaller only in size not in imagination or feeling, the Buddha sits into the earth. The steps and pedestal count for nothing. The great sitting weight bears down on the earth, heavy and pressing. It looks older than the hills and its slight features gentler and more placid than their contours. The soft shallow face has the weight of silence, a warm peace. Only the Buddha's hands are light. They rest folded and quiet with upturned palms, the thumbs and forefingers forming a figure eight, but they give life to the image, and save the seated mass from ponderance. The great, solid down-thrusting lines are broken by these hands which, crossing the settling curves of the body, preserve the statue's balance. It is a lost solitary Buddha sitting in an alien earth of which it forces itself to be part, solemn and sedate in its abrupt surroundings, which in turn emphasize the soft grandeur of its huge conception.

Around the statue nothing is quiet. From the buses pour batches of bullet-headed schoolboys, jumper-clad girls and excursions of sparse women and shirt-sleeved men. They range themselves in groups for photographs on the steps below the figure. They scramble up and pat the bronze, jostling and chattering. To the right is a row of stalls selling nuts and packets of dried seaweed, post cards and crude models of the Buddha. From a loudspeaker music blares, playing, while we were there, Sibelius' "Finlandia."

The Japanese are the most determined sightseers. Shrines and temples are always thronged with tourists, peering nervously about them, at the same time striding arrogantly, unsure of how to behave yet conscious always of history, and complacent in their certainty of the beauty of their heritage.

The tourists walk firmly as though on familiar ground and strew paper, cans and refuse carelessly behind them. It is ours, they seem to say, and it is the finest in the world. We can behave as we like.

But through the strutting, the importance of the history and the beauty strikes them and crumbles a part of them. In a shrine or temple they remember nervously their gods, and in a castle their lords. The fabric of respect bears down on them and humbles them. It is not the collapse of an "I'm-as-good-as-you" attitude in the face of something unsubduable. It is an acceptance of the rights of power; an acknowledgment of the system of hierarchy of which the Japanese are eager victims. It is a symbol of their character. First the purposeful pride in being Japanese, the atavistic feeling of being the divinely created rulers of the world united under a God Emperor and then the longing to sink into the obscurity of the mass, the willing victim's masochistic yearning for his proper station, the desire to subjugate individuality to the claims of an ordered society.

This dichotomy, among a hundred others, is omnipresent. It exists in all relationships—a contemptuous arrogance tempered by the desire to avoid all responsibility; to be subjected.

The hotel lay in the mountains about eight miles from the lake of Hakone and twenty miles from Mount Fuji. The hillsides were steep and characterless, covered with a near-tropical vegetation, enlivened only by flashes of azaleas and narrow waterfalls. It was not the true country of Japan but an isolated patch of lushness which defied cultivation. Within five miles on all sides was more typical scenery. So we waited for the car and spent our time trying to learn Japanese and

wandering about the precipitous village resort, as uncharac-
teristic as the countryside, with its souvenir stalls and expensive antique shops.

It was not the tourist season, the cherry blossom being
just over, but the hotel was full with the members of the
Leningrad State Orchestra who had had to move out of their
Tokyo hotel to make room for one thousand male athletes
in Japan for the Asian Games. They were friendly though
reserved, but one rather lonely figure with a knot of black
hair stood out among them. We seemed to run into him in
every shop and at all corners. Each time he would stop and
talk to us for a few moments. He told us of his house in
Leningrad and about his little daughter. In his eyes was
always a bemused saddened look and after a few moments
he would drift away without finishing what we were talking
about. He was somehow appealing.

We determined to buy a doll for his daughter and spent
some time choosing one which we thought different from
anything she could have seen, as colorful and lively as possible. We carried it with us in its box until we next met him.
It happened that this was late in the evening in the passage
just outside the main lounge of the hotel. For once he was
with a friend.

I handed him the box and said it was a small present for
his daughter. He jumped away from me and thrust the pack-
age back at me.

"No, no, I cannot take it."

I explained again that it was only a little thing for his
daughter, whereupon his companion turned sharply to me.

"He must not have it. We may not accept presents. We

don't want them. No presents. We want nothing. Give us nothing. Nothing."

Our friend was now edging away. "Room? Room?" he asked. The rooms in the hotel mostly had numbers, but a few, ours for one, were called by the names of flowers.

"Chrysanthemum," I said hopelessly, and he stared at me then went off down the passage. "Chrysanthemum," I called feebly at him. What could the Russian for chrysanthemum be? We went disconsolately to our room, fearing lest we should have compromised him.

Early in the morning, when we were still in bed, someone scratched rather than knocked at our door. I opened it and found the Russian looking stealthily up and down the corridor. I made him come in, and he stood near the door which he had shut quickly after him. For some time he stood there without speaking, merely shaking his head. At last he managed to ask me to draw down the blinds over the windows, which were at ground level looking over a small garden. I did so, and only then would he come out into the room.

"They might watch us," he said.

"Can you take the present now?"

"Yes, I want to. But you must take this." He smiled for the first time and gave me a small parcel in exchange and we both unwrapped our gifts. He had bought a small vase with a picture on it of a ship in full sail.

"The water reminds me of Leningrad," he said, "that is why I want you to have it. When you see the ship you will think of Leningrad. You must have, too, these pictures of Leningrad. It is my town, the most beautiful town in the world."

He sat down uneasily on my bed and showed me the booklet.

"My daughter will like the doll," he said, and from his pocket produced a photograph of a round-eyed little girl.

"But I must be careful, very careful." He then showed us his English phrase book.

"No, I cannot accept your invitation."

"No, I do not want your gift."

"No, I do not want to meet you again."

"No, you cannot come to my hotel."

"You see," he said, "*nyet, nyet, nyet*, everything is *nyet*. But we can remember. No one can say *nyet* to that."

He shook me firmly by the hand. Then, when I had looked to see that no one was in sight, he slipped out of the room. That morning the orchestra left.

It was a forlorn, irrelevant incident.

The car came and our orbit was extended beyond the dully beautiful hillsides which surrounded the hotel. We could now go into the real countryside of Japan and see for the first time its small fierce landscape, the sharp rocky contours of the mountains with, in between, little bites of valley shining green and neat with work. The familiar Japanese woodcuts do not lie. The simple fact that, after all, those spiky little prints with their improbable lines and twisted eccentric hills, their slanting threadlike rain and spiraled mists are not a stylized fancy but almost pure realism, is a surprise. A surprise which robs the drawings of their charm of invention by which they were before alone explicable. They can never again hold quite the same enchantment.

In the early morning the mists slide grayly over the valleys and creep into the gullies of the mountains like white ropes on the steep hillsides. The morning is the time when the landscape seems most like the prints. The hillsides hang in the air like a firmer continuation of the clouds. Everything is fluid, nothing earthbound. As the mists move and wander, so the land itself seems to change in shape. The rumpled contours of the mountains stretch restlessly up and down in the fashion of a rough sea. Nothing is permanent, nothing is definite, all is lightly sketched in, leaving solidity to the imagination. The color is a gray-green monochrome, taking its lead from the clouds and mists. The pine trees adding their spiky shapes to the sharp mountains give black-green outlines. The morning is a time of fleeting, unmarked beauty—the time which the Japanese feel represents most clearly their ideals. They are perhaps even a little sad when the rising sun begins to furnish the scene with color.

With the sun up, the land takes on the harsh reality of a grudging soil from which too many people must squeeze their living. The light reveals the pinched bitter terrain with great expanses of rock which will yield nothing, acres of heights upon which only a tree will grow, steep rushing rivers liable to flood, the fresh scars of earthquakes, woods flattened by searing winds—a countryside and a climate inimical to man's search for a home and a livelihood.

During the day the sun beats scorchingly into the depths of the steep valleys, showing up with a harsh dusty light the struggles against this most forbidding nature. Only 17 per cent of all the land in Japan can be cultivated and to look down into one of the valleys is to understand the precariousness of the life the Japanese lead; the industry, the sheer hard toil, that they must give in order to survive. You see how every minutest particle is used and worked with never a rest. There are no waste spaces. Nothing can lie fallow, and the houses of the villages are crammed tight together. Never more than a few square feet are given over to a garden. Paddy fields are divided only by thin strips of embankment to hold the water in. The telegraph poles are set on the actual roadways so as not to take an inch from the rice crops. No plots await development. The paddy fields themselves rise up from the foot of the valleys in terraces, clawed out of the hillsides until it is no longer possible to obtain even a few square inches of flat space. The farmer thinks it worth while to build a wall four feet high in order to obtain a tiny triangle of earth on which nine stalks of rice will grow. Before the houses there are no sidewalks. In the remoter villages it is possible to reach out from a car and touch the windows of the houses on both sides. There are no paths, no places to wander, nowhere to set a picnic. For playgrounds the schools have half an acre of bare asphalt. There are no rubbish dumps, there is no waste, there is no food to throw away for everyone needs every scrap which is set before him. There are no cans, as nearly everyone produces the food that he will eat and, if there were waste cans someone would have a use for them. There is no need for sanitation, for off the paddy fields rises the smell of human excrement, carefully saved as manure for the crops.

The rice crop is the only concern of the country people. In their formalized greetings, an inquiry after the other man's rice comes before questions about his family. It is on the rice crop that everyone's fate depends. It is the staple food in a way that no one who thinks of bread as being a staple food can possibly imagine. At every meal they eat rice—never less than two bowls, often more. Even the smartest dinner party always ends with two bowls of rice. Rice is used in the making of the little cakes which are given to any visitor. Rice is the base of the national drink of *sake*. Rice has been the food of the country for two thousand years. It was brought from Asia at a time when there was no form of writing in the country, yet there remains to this day a humbled form of animistic ritual attached to the production of rice. In the spring the paddy fields lie flooded and naked. Only the narrow strips of the dykes which divide them show above the water, giving them the appearance of acres of inundated foundations. Sowing begins in May. The seeds are prepared for weeks beforehand, and various rituals to please the gods are observed. These vary from place to place. Hideo Haga describes the planting which takes place in a village in Aichi prefecture.

The village bell rings at six o'clock in the morning and the villagers prepare to sow the seed by hand. The work may last till as late as nine o'clock at night. At that time a bamboo staff is planted in the middle of an irrigation ditch. Attached to it are sacred objects brought from a shrine in Nagoya city. The paddy is cleaned ceremonially by sprinkling salty water over the field with the branch of a tree. At the source where the water comes into the paddy field they put flowers and scatter toasted rice and even sometimes pour *sake*. For the god of the rice is supposed to come into the field with the water. The water almost becomes the god.

Rituals of this sort go on throughout the year as the fields change their appearance. By June the seedlings of rice have grown into thick close patches of vivid green. The color of the landscape has altered with the growing of the rice. In June the transplanting takes place. Each seedling is taken up and replanted in the larger fields, each plant separated exactly from the other by a given distance. The whole operation is so precise that it makes one think of horticulture rather than of agriculture. The work is hard, and it is enlivened by the singing of ritual songs and the performance of other rites which help to give the workers a feeling of greater significance in their labor. The effect on the landscape for a short while is rather surprising. Where before there were great thick slabs of green there is water once again with little bright tufts like a buttoned Victorian chair. But soon the green returns as the plants grow bigger. Throughout the summer the work does not lessen. Farmers fuss over each plant like a rose grower, pressing it down so that it shall not float away, standing it up so that its stalk shall grow straight, even delousing it. The fear of insects is very great. Everywhere in Japan there are *mushiokuri* ceremonies which are supposed to ward off pests. Haga again describes a strange one in the same prefecture, where the farmers fashion a large stallion and rider out of straw. The representation is very complete, even down to an enormous scrotum filled with seedlings. This effigy is carried round the fields at dusk to the accompaniment of much bell ringing and drum beating. This time it is the straw horse and rider which is the god of rice. Nevertheless at the end of the parade this god is burned, which mysteriously turns it into a devil.

The rice ears ripen to a dull brown, taking from the valleys the live strong green and replacing it with a somber tone, for rice never achieves the rich golden color of wheat or barley. The harvest takes place roughly in October, though this varies according to the district. The crop is not collected into sheaves, but hung on poles to dry in the wind. In some places there are many single poles about three feet from the ground; in others they put the crop on high frameworks so that when you come upon a valley from above it looks almost as though a huge game of dominoes were taking place in the fields below. At harvesttime there are more rituals. Indeed the ceremonies may go on even after the crop is safely in, many of them services outdoors in honor of the gods that are often to be seen in the paddies—small stone figures frequently very phallic in shape, which are prayed to throughout the year. The New Year too is important for placating the gods of rice. At this time the Japanese farmers make a quite particularly disgusting lump of food, made out of pounded rice, all sticky and clammy. This is eaten on New Year's Day to the accompaniment of a great many observances.

Whereas fifty years ago the rice paddies lay empty through the winter, except where they grew the *tatami* rushes for the thick mats to cover the floor of every Japanese building, science from the West has brought the possibility of double crops. These were known in the south before, but now all over Japan winter wheat and other things use the land the whole year around. The increase in population, however, means that this does not necessarily give the Japanese farmer a higher standard of living. It means, too, more work. Until the new crops were introduced the hard cold winter was a time of comparative leisure. Much of the land lay peaceful and delicately beautiful under snow and the villagers could work on their houses, their slender diet being just enough to keep them warm indoors. Now, with little more to eat they work in the winter fields as hard as in the summer. And if they eat other things besides rice from sheer necessity, rice still remains the food which they prefer. They would never dream of leaving a grain in the bottom of a bowl, nor of eating only one bowl of rice, for one bowl is what is given to the dead.

CHAPTER FOUR

HOUSE HUNTING

A<small>FTER</small> a few days we drove on to Kyoto, thumping over the wretched surface of the Tokaido Highway and, arriving, found it almost as great a disappointment as Tokyo had been. Here was the seat of Japanese culture, the city which had been the capital of Japan from 794 until the Meiji restoration in 1868. It should, I felt, have combined the charms of Oxford and Florence. Indeed its setting is strongly reminiscent of Florence, for it is surrounded by high tree-covered hills, and through its center runs a broad attractive river. But instead of the delights of a university town in Europe, we were greeted by something more like a ramshackle boom town in the American west. The color is the same brown and gray which swamps every Japanese town. There are few buildings higher than three stories, and those that there are, are characterless copies of what to us is by-pass architecture of the nineteen-thirties.

The city is a cluster of irregular wooden houses. None of them is painted, and there can be no more depressing material for town planning than naked wood, which after a few years takes on a drabness matched only by cracking concrete.

A long time must pass before one discovers the character of Kyoto. It can never have for Western eyes the appeal of an Italian or French or Spanish medieval city even when they, like Kyoto, have had added to them the grueling demands of modern industry. For us to be pleased aesthetically it is necessary to see a whole overt demand made upon our sensibilities. We like avenues and squares, crescents and terraces. For the Japanese this is almost meaningless. They may acquire a slightly perverse taste for them, but *au fond* they can never find them anything but vulgar. There is, too, the economic factor. Rapid, unchecked expansion does not make for beauty. Japanese taste is confined to the solitary object. By tradition they like to see but one thing, and to come upon that one thing by simulated chance. A room will never have more than one picture. It is put certainly in a place of honor—the *tokonoma,* common to every Japanese room—but, as often as not, you will be unable to see it as you come into the room. So a beautiful temple will be hidden behind a wall and among trees, so the most elegant houses will be invisible from the road. Almost by tradition any Japanese man will be inclined to decry the national pastime of cherry-blossom viewing. He will join the hordes of his countrymen who go out to see the astonishing flowering trees, and he will ooh and aah at them. But privately he will tell you it is not the great remarkable splashes of color streaking the countryside which appeal to him. All that is a little obvious, he will say. What he goes to see each year is one tree—perhaps one branch of that tree, the particular formation of which arouses in him some special emotion. And he will like to catch that branch just at the moment when the

first petal falls from it, and the perfect image which he has
treasured all the year begins to break. And anyhow, he will
tell you, he really prefers quite another branch—that of a
maple tree fading in the autumn.

It is a strange thing to contemplate the impact on these
people of what is virtually a new conception—the exhibition.
They go, it is true, to see exhibitions, and move from object
to object with assiduous energy. I am not sure what the feelings are of someone who has been trained from youth to be
satisfied with looking at one beautifully drawn ideogram
hanging on the wall, at having to digest in one voluptuous
hour a hundred different aspects or interpretations of art. It
may be that it will cause them to overcome their total indif-
ference to the external aspect of their towns and that in fifty
years' time their architecture will take on some cohesion.

However, our minds were made up and after the first pang
of disappointment we set about looking for a house. We were
staying at the Miyako Hotel. It was, as far as comfort went,
the usual travesty of a Western hotel which we had come to
expect. Japanese taste, while so restrained and perfect in its
own context, develops a riotous inconsequence when at-
tempting to emulate foreign style. The rooms were bare and
decorated in artless gray. The huge dining room was like an
overgrown log cabin, and the bar with vast round pillars of
glazed brick would have been suitable only as the main
lavatory at Karnak.

After a few days we forgot the horrors of its ugliness in
amazement at the kindness of the staff. We had not yet got
used to the passionate and absorbed interest which people
would take in one's affairs. It is inconceivable that in any

other country the people behind the desk in an hotel could so identify themselves with one's problems. It might also be said that we had not yet understood the confused web of obligation which can bind people to you in Japan. This is not to deny their kindness, but it was only later that we came to appreciate that there are a thousand situations in which you can place other people from which they have no escape save that of unthinkable rudeness. For whatever cause, though in their case I think it was pure kindness, my family and I became the objects of unending concern to the three chief people at the reception desk. There was the usual resistance to our doing anything out of the ordinary and, for their clientele, renting a house came well within this specification. It was the same reluctance that we had met in the travel bureau, with the two professors, even in the long-exiled members of our embassy who had absorbed Japanese attitudes—a reluctance grounded in an almost obsessive conventionality. To do anything which offends against precedent causes them to feel an irrepressible discomfort. There is in all things a ceremonial to be observed. There is the ever-present suspicion of being an individual.

The performance of finding a house was much more complicated than we had imagined. There appeared to be no estate agents of any sort. Never do you see a signboard outside a house saying TO LET or FOR SALE. The idea that somebody might drop in, a total stranger, and ask to be shown over your house is beyond contemplation. Any arrangement of this sort can only be done through the offices of friends or friends of friends.

Again we tried the tourist bureau and their answer to our

problem was not to send us a list of possible houses but rather to send us a Mr. Shimamura, who was understood to have a wide acquaintanceship in the town. Each morning he would come and see me with whatever news he had managed to gather together the previous day. This would never be put to me in the form of a statement that he had a house for me to see. Instead he would say, "My cousin has a friend whom I should like to meet." "Has he a house?" I would ask. "Ah, that I do not know. My cousin says that we might enjoy meeting." The next day he would have got a stage further. He would have met the cousin's friend who, it would appear, worked in an office with someone whose aunt might have news for Mr. Shimamura. The quality of the news was never disclosed. Mr. Shimamura worked tirelessly arranging a succession of meetings over cups of green tea, picking up threads which he hoped would lead eventually to the discovery of a house. So involved were the negotiations that I don't think we ever actually saw any house that he had found. As the thread to each house became slowly unraveled a little more information about it would be given us, but it would often take as many as five days before we even heard how many rooms there were, so that all his time might be fruitlessly spent in pursuit of house with no bathroom. The operation would then have to start all over again.

The hotel staff, however, were to a certain degree more ambitious and less secretive, perhaps as a result of their constant dealings with Westerners, but even with them the formalities could by no means be brushed aside.

Our days, as well as Mr. Shimamura's, were taken up with a confused succession of polite little tea parties at the end of

which we would have understood nothing of how the business in hand had progressed, as the conversation seemed to
us to have been devoted almost exclusively to perpetual inquiry as to what I was attached to and as to what were my
impressions of Japan. Any direct questions we might have
put were always greeted with sympathetic little giggles by
whoever was translating, and we noticed that quite long
questions appeared to be translated by remarkably few
syllables in Japanese. We suspected that in fact our sentences
were not translated at all, and when later we came to know
the language we realized that this was so. Direct, precipitous
questions of the sort that we were likely to ask were considered far too rude and abrupt to pass on. Our interpreters
were always so jealous of our honor that they would always
rather protract the negotiations by several days than have it
thought that we did not know how to behave.

At last one of the hotel clerks told us that a succession of
little meetings had got us to the point where we could go and
see a house attached to a temple, in one of the main com-
pounds of the Zen sect of Buddhism in Kyoto.

The compound, known as Daitokuji, lies in the northwest
corner of the city. From the main road very little can be seen,
but as you go in from the hustling, untidy street through a
huge gateway you find yourself transported suddenly into a
world that has barely changed for three hundred years.
There are twenty-three temples arranged in a haphazard
pattern, varying in size from the main one, which covers
about the same area as a large English country house, to
quite small ones such as the one we went to see, which was
little more than an extended bungalow. Each has its garden

surrounded by a wall about ten feet high and, in the wall, a roofed gateway with heavy wooden doors. We went through one of the smaller ones and up a little path flanked on either side with bushes and stunted pine trees. It is part of the ingenious effect of Japanese gardening that such a path, together with the bushes on either side of it, is often no wider than a broad passage, and yet the impression given is one not exactly of space but of complete privacy and isolation.

On the highest step of the temple a monk was waiting for us. He was for a Japanese tall and impressive, in a blue and black gauzy kimono which he wore over his white robe. His head was shaven and underneath his bald skull his face looked hollow, with a convincing asceticism. He had a strange deep voice as he greeted us in Japanese. He led us into the temple, which was indistinguishable from an ordinary Japanese house except that the unpolished woods of the beams were of a fine quality and that here and there stood little carvings and ceramics and many of the door screens were painted with exquisite landscapes.

We sat down and drank the tea, and chatted aimlessly through our interpreter. Then the monk, Kobori San, surprised me by taking us straight away to the house adjoining the temple. It was a recently built annex having about four rooms, completely Japanese in style, with its own little strip of garden eight feet wide. Kobori took us around it very briskly, explaining all the time that it would be extremely inconvenient for us. Accustomed by now to Japanese manners, I decided that this was merely the usual parade of self-deprecation. I kept on assuring him that it was exactly what we wanted. The more I did so the more he bustled us around, so that it was only at the last moment that I noticed the house had no water. We put a few tentative questions about this and were surprised to find them adequately translated and properly answered. It would cost, he told me, a matter of six dollars to have some water put in.

We went back to the temple and Kobori showed us around with a great display of pride. To our eyes it was a pinched place, with rather few, small rooms, built around a minute scrubby garden consisting of a few azalea bushes, some bamboo and a number of flat stones set in a carpet of moss. We viewed this garden from all sides. The whole thing could not have been bigger than two billiard tables. Kobori explained that the temple was a national treasure and that the garden had been designed in about 1598 by Kobori Enshu, an ancestor of our host and one of Japan's most famous landscape gardeners. We then sat down and had more tea and suddenly Kobori, who had affected to understand none of my questions about the house, broke into English. He was a remarkably vivid talker and, when we pressed him to tell us about his life in the monastery, he launched readily into a description of his family and circumstances.

He came, he told us, from a long line of rich feudal lords who had owned a castle some eighty miles from Kyoto at a time when the nobility had been closely connected with the development of Zen Buddhism. His ancestors had built this temple and it had remained in the family ever since. They owned, too, the temple next door, of which his brother was now the abbot. They seemed to have been rather an erratic family, and at one time the chief Kobori had killed at a whim many of his *samurai*. This was considered such a dreadful deed that most of the family had had to change their name. The direct descendants of the murderer were supposed to have a devil in them, and Kobori told us that one of his cousins always has some hideous dream just before going to sleep. When he comes to stay with Kobori, he insists on sleeping next to him and Kobori always sees agonized looks on his face just before he falls asleep. I asked him if he believed in this spell, whereupon he offered the surprisingly Western explanation that it was probably due to simple fear instilled by parents saying, "You must not be like your wicked great-great-great-grandfather."

Once embarked on telling us about himself Kobori was disinclined to stop until he had exhausted the ramifications of his father's family and found it well received. He then embarked on that of his mother. She, he said, was descended from the Imperial family—as far as I could understand it, the Emperor Meiji. "The Emperor kept an official Empress in Tokyo and another wife in Kyoto." (The Emperor Meiji was the only one to whom this could have applied, for until his restoration the Emperors had all lived in Kyoto, the country being governed by the Shogun in Tokyo.) Kobori said that the Emperor's children by his Kyoto wife or wives were treated as ordinary citizens and usually became monks or nuns. "They are supposed to have a particular kind of face—not flat, but oval like an egg with nose and eyes. I have it," said Kobori, "the Emperor has it. A most aristocratic face." His face in fact was not like an egg; nor, indeed, is the Emperor's, to which incidentally it bore little resemblance. The whole of Kobori's story, I felt, had to be taken with a grain of salt. But by this time he was determined that we should hear all of it. He drew a picture of himself as a young, carefree aristocrat who had gone to study the psychology of religion under the great exponent of Zen for Westerners, Dr. Suzuki. As a result of his influence he had gone to train in a monastery in Gifu Prefecture. "It was on one side of a hill. On the other side lay a Catholic monastery. The bells of the two monasteries competed all through the day but at different hours until at six o'clock in the evening they met with a great clang when we started meditation and the Catholics did goodness knows what. One day on the hillside I met a Catholic priest who took me to his cell and gave me an enormous loaf of bread which two friends and I ate for three days. It had no taste. It was very odd food for Zen monks but we were always hungry, especially in the evening."

"I thought privation—no food, drink or sleep—had no virtue in Zen," my wife said.

"It has no particular virtue," said Kobori, "but in monasteries we live very simply and in the winter we were very cold. Hunger and cold are great aids to meditation. I have always noticed that monks drop off to sleep after breakfast. But sleep is good. The students who get enough don't have to be kept awake with sticks during their meditation of only one hour a day."

Kobori's devotions were soon interrupted, for he was called up, as monks were not exempt. He joined the cavalry and found in military service a quality which appealed both to his religious and his national feelings. "I liked being just a piece of paper, having no identity, just something which could be moved about or used in whatever way they liked.

We used to be told that it was easier to get us than a horse, which cost six hundred yen while we only needed a post card." The war seemed to mean little to him, except in his gratification at finding himself only a cipher. His memories of it seemed to consist of two rather incongruous incidents. "I remember," he said, "and it is perhaps the memory of the cavalry which I love best, one night when two hundred horsemen moved off to a new encampment. They were not men, nor horses, but an endless stream of sparks flashing in the dark. Sparks, just a long like of sparks. That is all we were."

His other memory was of listening to foreign broadcasts, which was part of his job. "Oh, it was funny."

"Propaganda, you thought?"

"No, the music, not the news. I loved the music."

He seemed to have noticed nothing of battles, but merely to have enjoyed the humbling effect, which he regarded as good for him, and the unexpected pleasures of listening to jazz. It was hard to get him to talk about politics. I asked him whether he felt that democracy would catch on in Japan or whether the system of hierarchy was too deeply ingrained. "Democracy, or anyhow equality, is old in Japan. We believe that that glass and that teacup are equal in being what they are. They are different, but in having their own identity they are equal."

"That," I said, "is surely a most dangerous attitude—one which can be used to excuse any suppression or injustice."

"Ah, you talk about politics, economics. I like to leave politicians and economists to get on with their job."

"Even if it means you are suppressed?"

"I hope I won't be—that no one will be. But I don't mind if I am a beggar. Western people consider too much the past and the future. We are sitting here now, we three—we are our own society and we should taste the moment. It does not matter what you have done, or what is to come—we should live just this moment. It does not matter if you are a beggar or the Emperor—I treat you just the same way. This moment now is here and it is the same moment in New York. The places are different, but underneath it is the same. Consider yesterday—I read of a bathyscaphe going down off the Japanese coast. At the surface the fish life is unique to the Japanese sea, but deep down, at thirty hundred feet—or was it meters?—I dare say meters—the sea was the same, and the life was the same as at thirty hundred meters in the Mediterranean. So it is with people. We should live our own lives. Politics should be left to a world government."

"But you haven't answered my question," I said.

"No, I haven't," he replied.

There is a curious unconcern amongst Zen monks which at first sight makes one think that it is purely selfish religion. All direct questions that one puts to them are answered with skillful parallels. We asked him what *koan* (Zen meditation puzzle) he was working on.

"There was once a Zen master called Ju. He was busy cutting firewood and he made a high, high pile. Then suddenly, when he threw on a log, the pile collapsed. The priest said, 'When I hear a foreign sound it is not different. When the dust flies up from the pile of wood it is not dust.' And he was reminded of his awakening. Well, we are told by another Zen master of Ju's awakening. Ju once went to a palace where he was given everything he could want. But Ju felt that something was missing. What was it? That is what I am meditating on."

"What do you do when you are satisfied that you know?"

"You go to your master and tell him. But if you have any doubt, that is no good. It is the strength of your conviction which counts. The answers for different people are different. It may be one thing for an American and another thing for a Japanese, but you must know that your answer is right. You don't even have to tell the master. He knows from the way you say 'good morning' if you have found the answer."

I pointed out that this system might lead to abuse if the student were not wholly serious.

"In our institute," said Kobori, "we can tell by the way a person sits if he is serious. Too-intelligent people's heads droop forward—the sportsman's falls back. The person with true understanding sits just so. We have spoken very frankly, and sat here for three hours exactly. Good-by, take care of yourselves."

It may have been that my head lolled backward or forward, but whatever the reason, the next morning over yet another cup of green tea I was told by a friend of a friend of the monk's that the water would cost $150 to install. For all their philosophizing, Zen monks are sharper and more direct in business than most other Japanese. I later found out that Kobori, quite apart from the affair of the water, had been asking at least double the fair market price for his house.

CHAPTER FIVE

THE INN

Eventually, we gave up in despair and were persuaded to move into an inn which was recommended by one of our friends at the reception desk in the hotel. Even this took a great deal of palaver. It was an inn at which no foreigner had ever before stayed, and it appeared in none of the guide books, but the owner had apparently agreed in principle, through a few cousins and friends, that he would take the risk. It was not surprising that it was little known to the public, for it was situated in the unfashionable southeast corner of the city and extremely hard to find. One turned off the main ring road which runs around Kyoto, up a little street full of shops and wooden houses. The street rose sharply up a hill for about two hundred yards and ended in a rather decrepit, little-used Shinto shrine. To one side of the forecourt of the shrine led a narrow path. One followed it and suddenly, after only twenty yards, one seemed to have reached pure countryside. The path led to a wooden bridge across a deep gorge filled by trees, with a small stream running thirty feet below the bridge. On the other side steep steps had been cut into the hillside, climbing up to a cluster

69

of two or three houses. On the right was the inn, called the Taiko (the Drum). The entrance from the pathway was through an impressive-looking gate set in a high wooden fence. Inside was a small cobbled space fringed with azalea bushes and, set at an angle, was the front door. Asymmetry is an important part of Japanese design. Hardly ever would you find a gateway leading into a square yard with a front door facing the gate centrally. The object is always to make it seem a little more spacious and to avoid the obvious.

On the first day we went in through the front door to the concrete-floored hall at the end of which was the usual high step into the house. The concrete space had just been sluiced over with water, as is always done when visitors are expected. We stepped out of our shoes and into the pairs of slippers waiting on the step. The master of the inn was there to meet us. For a Japanese he was a large, burly figure, with graying hair and an unexpectedly jovial face. His name was Ishida. We went straight away into a remarkably attractive room open on two sides—on one looking down over the gorge across which we had just come, and on the other over about an acre of garden so arranged and contrived that although we were nearly at the top of the hill we were quite unable to see out of it. Yet unlike Kobori's garden at his temple one did not feel cramped or shut in.

Over cups of green tea we discussed only the weather, our journey and, as always, our impressions of Japan. This last subject seems to be something more than the usual required courtesies of the first twenty minutes of any Japanese conversation. It is a question put to one over and over again, and to which all Japanese seem to require a reassuring answer.

It is as though they felt themselves to be in some way freaks, and they needed to be told on each occasion that each new foreigner had managed to overcome his surprise at them. They suffer more than any other nation from an abiding national self-consciousness.

Eventually the master of the inn asked if we would like to see some rooms. There seemed quite a number for us to choose from. There were no other guests and so we wandered from room to room, trying to decide which had the nicest view over the garden. It just so happened that none of them was particularly convenient. The choice lay in the end between a large room in the main building, in which case our child would have been in another rather far away, or a quite separate little cabin in the garden with two minute rooms, really too small. Seeing us unable to decide, Ishida San very kindly offered to move out of his own room, which had a convenient little room leading off it suitable for Sebastian. A great discussion went on through our interpreter, for we obviously felt we could not accept this arrangement which would put the innkeeper to such trouble. But it soon became plain that, if we were going to stay, he would insist on giving up his own room and so it was settled. It is some measure of Japanese disregard for personal possessions that the move took him under ten minutes.

We settled down into these two rooms which he had sacrificed and started to live a totally Japanese life. The arrangement was that we should live *en pension* for a flat rate of two hundred and fifty dollars a month.

Almost nothing was familiar. Our breakfast would be brought us in our room by Yaoko San, the chief maid in the inn. She was an extremely pretty girl of about twenty-four who spoke no English, and indeed we could communicate with no one in the inn except by signs. The breakfast on the first morning was something of a shock. It consisted of thick silty soup made out of beans and tasting of nothing so strongly as manure. This was accompanied with miniature fish dipped in caramel and bowls of rice and some peculiarly bitter pickled vegetables. After that morning it was the only break with Japanese life that we allowed ourselves—a proper English breakfast, or anyway a fried egg which was carefully allowed to get cold before it was brought to us, a thick travesty of toast and some Nescafé. After breakfast we would have a bath. This again was perhaps not strictly Japanese behavior, for they always had their bath in the evening before dinner, but as dinner was at six we found this so cut into the day that we instituted the morning bath. But it was a proper Japanese one.

The bathroom was a few yards down the passage from our room. The room was tiled all over the floor and up the walls to about waist height. In one corner was the bath itself, a wooden tub four feet square and about three feet deep. It was heated by a fire directly underneath it, which was fed through a hole outside in the garden. The principle of a Japanese bath is that you wash all over outside the tub and then, having rinsed off all the soap by pouring water over yourself with special wooden bowls, you get in, quite clean, and soak. In this way it is possible for a whole family to use the same water, though the lastcomers may find the bath beginning to be a bit shallow. In ordinary Japanese families, the father has his bath first, followed by all male members of the family, then by the females and lastly the servants. Our bath was a private one, which we shared with no one. But when I went away the master would never think it worth lighting the bath for Martha, and she had to take her turn in the large bath far away down the corridor used by Ishida and the servants of the inn—and she had to have it in the evening.

The great problem of the bath was temperature. We always had to add quantities of cold water before we could get into it. Later on, when we had our own house, we had our bath in the evening, or rather, late at night. The servants would have theirs about six. They would then cover it with a lid and leave it for us. When we got to it at about ten or eleven it would still be absolutely impossible for us to put our hands in the water. We found that after a year's training we could, at a pinch, get into the bath at about 112 or 113 degrees Fahrenheit, though 110 was really as hot as we enjoyed it. This is about eight degrees hotter than an average bath in England. I calculated that the servants must be having theirs at about 118 degrees. In the winter one came to be thankful for this heat, for all bathrooms have to have an outside wall so that the fire beneath may be fed and there was no means, once you were in, of making the bath warmer.

During the day the same room in which we had slept served as a sitting room. It was plain and bare. The floor was covered with eight *tatami* mats. The size of any room in Japan is judged by the number of mats. They are about an inch and a half thick, and all of a uniform size—approximately six feet by three feet—so that any room is bound to be in size a multiple of the area of one mat or in some cases half a mat. The coarse underpart of the mat is covered with a very finely woven surface of the same *tatami* reed. They are very fragile, and for this reason, as well as for cleanliness the Japanese never wear shoes in the house. The thin surface of the mats is easily torn, so they do not even wear slippers on the *tatami*, but keep them merely for the wooden passages outside. The color of the mats is a natural pale straw, and the only decoration on the floor apart from the texture of the reeds is the braiding—usually black, but sometimes red, brown or even patterned—which binds the edge of each mat.

The natural color of the floor was followed out in the walls and ceiling. The walls were of plain plaster divided into segments, of approximately the same size as the mats, by narrow strips of unpainted wood. And the ceiling too was natural wood, with thin beams slightly raised, following the same pattern as the braiding of the mats on the floor. The doors were sliding panels covered in paper of a nondescript color. These again echoed the shape of the mats, though they were a little wider and a little lower. Along the whole of one side of the room was a window with sliding glass doors in wooden frames. The matting stopped about three feet short of the window, and at that point there were again sliding doors, this time made of translucent paper framed in tiny panes, which afforded some privacy from anyone passing in the garden. The window led straight out into the garden, so that you could step down from the little three-foot veranda first on to a large boulder and then on to a path of irregular flagstones which threaded at random through the shrubs.

In one corner of the room was a little raised platform of wood about an inch high on which stood a vase with one flower in it. And above that was a hanging scroll with three ideograms on it which read:

> "A baby sleeping
> A cherry blossom falls on its cheek."

There was no other decoration, no furniture, no color.

This was the room in which we lived by day and night, using it as a bedroom, a sitting room, in the Japanese manner. The plain austerity of the room was satisfying and, because of the window, there was no feeling that it was bare or forlorn. The garden coming, as it did, virtually into the house, provided the room with color and decoration, almost indeed furnished it.

There was a little four-mat room next door in which our child, Sebastian, slept, separated from us by only a sliding door. This was considered very peculiar by the Japanese, who from the day that they are born never sleep without some companion. At first they sleep with their mothers, and then as more children appear in the family with their brothers and sisters. It is quite common for brothers to sleep side by side until they are married.

When lunch- or dinnertime came, a low red lacquer table, about eight inches high, was brought in and set in the middle of the room. We would sit around it on thin cushions. Yaoko would then bring the food. Japanese cooking requires some time to get used to. At first we could hardly bear to eat anything that was put before us, and as a result I have a slightly unjust memory of the food we had in the inn. It seemed at that time that I had never eaten anything so disgusting, and yet I now realize that, by the time I left Japan, I had come to regard as quite delicious the very dishes which had revolted me so much for the first few months. Even quite good food consists of very little more than various kinds of fish done in unexpected ways, scraps of duck or chicken usually with the skin still clinging to them, a variety of vegetables, the inevitable bowls of rice, plainly boiled until it becomes a slightly glutinous mass easy to pick up on chopsticks. There were rarely any courses—everything was brought in together, both hot and cold things, sweet things and bitter things. Soup came in with the rest, but was not usually drunk until the end, just before the rice. There was never very much of one particular dish, so one would pick at a piece of raw fish, then a morsel of the entrails of sea slug, followed by some rather sloppy bean curd which it was extremely difficult to keep on the chopsticks. *Sukiyaki*, which seems to be the only Japanese dish which has been adopted abroad, is one of which one quickly tires, particularly as many people give *sukiyaki* parties at which one eats nothing else whatever but goes on stuffing oneself with the thin slices of beef accompanied by stewed chrysanthemum leaves and something which resembles an anaemic worm until one can literally eat no more.

Traditional Japanese cuisine has nothing fried except for one dish, which is called *tempura*, perhaps the most attractive dish for foreigners. It consists of some kind of fish, usually shrimp, dipped in batter then fried in deep fat, and vegetables, often artichokes or baby summer squashes, treated in the same way. It is slightly disappointing to find that this dish and even its name is a sixteenth-century Portu-

guese importation. The fact that they eat no fat of any sort
has two effects on the Japanese. First they remain remarkably spare and thin. It is extremely unusual to see a fat
person for even rice is, unexpectedly, not fattening. The
second is to give them an almost ludicrous lack of resistance
to alcohol. They get drunk quicker than any other nation in
the world, and it has the most startling effect on their faces,
for the blood seems to rush unhindered to their cheeks. I
remember one young girl coming to lunch with us and having only one glass of *sake*. Within a matter of minutes she
was giggling and patting her cheeks, which is the customary
gesture as they feel the blood mounting. She had to drink
seven glasses of water before she was satisfied that she had
sufficiently diluted the alcohol. *Sake* is, as it happens, not
very strong, containing approximately the same amount of
alcohol as a good bottle of wine. It is served hot in tiny cups
that hold less than a small egg cup. After nine of these almost
any Japanese man will be quite transformed, whereas a
foreigner will often have to drink about thirty of these
thimblefuls before he is aware of any change. I have many
times sat through a dinner with a maid kneeling beside me
pouring away for all she was worth while her eyes grew
wider and wider in insulted disbelief.

As I say, we grew used to our meals and always appreci-
ated the extraordinary elaborateness with which everything
was prepared in order to make up for there not being much
of anything. Each kind of food was arranged fastidiously on
its own small dish. At the end of a meal for four one could
often count about eighty plates and bowls, some of which
might only have contained one radish, a gherkin and a sprig

of parsley laid together in an effective pattern. Accustomed
though we became to the food itself, we never got used to
the fact that everything got cold. It was once explained to
me that this was considered in the old days to be chic, the
reason being that the Emperor's kitchen was so far from the
living quarters that nothing could be kept warm on the open
plates on which everything is served. It was poor consolation
for a congealed fried egg. Throughout the meal Yaoko would
kneel beside me, attracting my attention to untouched dishes
in case I had missed them, or pouring out thimblefuls of *sake*
and joining in the conversation whenever she thought fit.
Martha was always left to fend for herself.

In ordinary Japanese life they keep very early hours. It
was with great difficulty that we persuaded them that we
didn't want our dinner until seven. It was always cooked at
six in any case, and not long after it was over Yaoko would
come and tell us that it was time for bed. We used to manage
to put this off for a little while, but by ten she would become
positively anxious. The red table would have been cleared
away and the girl would go to the sliding cupboards in which
was kept our bedding. This consisted of two heavy quilts
which were laid on the floor and another one to go over us.
The Japanese are eccentric about temperature. In winter
they make strangely little provision against the cold, a whole
room being heated by only a few sticks of charcoal. But
at night they seem to require a prodigious weight of bedclothes. The overquilt—summer one, that is—weighed about
as much as three blankets. They usually sleep under these
even when the temperature is about eighty degrees. In
winter they use two, much heavier ones. The quilts laid on

the floor strike one at first as being very hard. To start with one seems to be all hip, but after a while one adjusts to the fact that there is no give and becomes extremely grateful for the fact that wherever one sleeps one is sure of an absolutely flat bed and never has to tussle with lumps and dips.

We moved to the *Taiko* in June—the rainy season—and the mosquitoes were ferocious. Each night Yaoko would light an evil-smelling coil of green incense. She would then seal all the windows and doors to the garden, so that we would always have to get up and open everything up again—a habit at which she would express astonishment every morning, but nothing we said would dissuade her from doing it. It was a respected ritual of her duty.

Such was our way of life, and, except for the fact that the room was clean and the food well above the average standard, we were living in virtually the same style as the vast majority of the people of Japan. There is very little to distinguish the room of a poor man from that of a rich man. The rich man's house will be cleaner, the wood of the beams and the door posts will be of a better wood, though this is apparent only to someone who knows a good deal about it. The poor man's room will be smaller—even as few as four mats—but both will have *tatami* on the floor, the poor man's a little worn. Both will have the shelf for the treasured picture or scroll of calligraphy with the pot of one, two or three flowers beneath it. Neither will have any furniture, neither will have any paint. The rich man may have glass where the poor has paper. The rich man may have a servant to do some of the work of the poor man's wife. The poor man may share his room with four people, whereas the rich may be alone with his wife. But in quality their lives will be the same. The rich man will avoid all show of his riches, and the poor one will strive to conceal his poverty. There is, in sum, a cult of uniformity, a singleness of attitude which creates a common meeting ground for all men, an at-first-glance classless society. There is, too, a drab, suffocating lack of individuality and, in the outsider, a fierce longing for a glimmer of expression.

During the month that we stayed there nobody else ever took a room in the inn. It was hard to find out how the place paid. Perhaps the fact that it was the rainy season, and on the whole people do not travel much at that time meant that it was a quiet period, though nothing suggested that the inn was ever busy. The only other visible source of income which the proprietor had was a number of evening parties given by businessmen. There was an exceptionally large room at one end of the inn—thirty-six mats, that is to say, thirty-six feet long by eighteen feet wide. At about half past five the guests would begin to arrive and would all have a bath together in the large bathroom beyond the reception room. A little later the geisha girls would come—never the businessmen's wives. There would be a large dinner and afterward the geishas would dance and sing to the *samisen,* a three-stringed instrument about four feet long with a round flat body which produces a sound like a mournful guitar. Fortunately for us these parties would break up at about eleven o'clock, for they were noisy enough until then.

Ishida never seemed to do anything. Some days he would just disappear in the little car which he owned, with the announcement that he was going to Osaka, but he never spoke of having any express business there. But on most days he would lie stretched out on the floor in the room next door to the kitchen playing for hours on end a game called Go, played on a board with three hundred and eighty-one squares.

He was a large man somehow epitomizing laziness as he reclined there on the mats, his figure barely covered by his blue and white summer kimono, white pants showing where the kimono parted and huge feet with agile toes bent back as he played. At each move his toes would wiggle and he would clap the piece down on the board with an exulting cry, apparently designed to goad his opponent. This opponent was supposedly the gardener, though I never saw him working very industriously at that task. Occasionally he would wander about plucking a few dead heads off the azaleas, but his son did all the work and I think he was merely employed to provide someone for Ishida to play against.

Besides the two Go players there were only Yaoko and an elderly rather indignant cook, and sometimes another maid who took over from Yaoko when she was out. On the other hand, the kitchen was always packed with aunts, cousins and other sundry relations and friends of each member of the staff. Ishida had at one time been married, but whether he was divorced or a widower or merely separated from his wife we never found out. However, when any members of the staff or their friends were indignant about something and came to talk to us about it they used to refer to Yaoko, of whom they were all jealous, as "the master's second wife." Second wife nearly always means mistress, for divorce is comparatively uncommon and it is unusual for anyone to marry again after his wife has died. Widows and widowers are looked upon as of very dubious value in the marriage market, though a girl who is still unmarried at thirty is quite likely to accept a widower in despair.

We decided that we needed a nurse to look after Sebastian while we were out, and asked Ishida if he knew of anybody. He rather surprised us by suggesting that we should advertise in one of the Japanese newspapers, considering that we should get one much cheaper than if we tried in the English-language ones. He drafted some sort of an advertisement inviting anyone who was interested in the job to call one afternoon at three o'clock.

From about two-thirty onward we heard a constant shuffling of feet down the passage outside our room to which we paid little attention. It wasn't until three o'clock that we realized what had happened. Then Yaoko led me down the passage to the large reception room, where I found forty women waiting to be interviewed. They all sank down in one deep sweeping bow, some of them even kneeling and touching their heads to the ground. They were of all ages, half of them dressed in kimonos and the other half in Western clothes. I had no idea what to do so I bowed too, as politely as possible, and fled back to our room. It seemed quite impossible to choose among them, so we told Yaoko to bring them to us one by one. We saw first of all, those who spoke English, but mostly they were either girls who had picked it up while working as hostesses in bars, or who had worked for Americans and had in consequence a rather brash disappointing attitude. After interviewing a dozen I asked to see some who couldn't speak English. It was an infinitely laborious task trying to communicate with them through Yaoko in a mixture of her English and our Japanese. It was additionally hard because Yaoko had quite different ideas from ours as to the sort of person we wanted. Having understood that we did not want a coffee-bar girl she decided we must mean something dug up from Japanese history. I remember one particular old crone that Yaoko was very keen about. She had a white painted face normally associated with *kabuki* actors and all over her arms were large, rather livid scars, circular in shape, as if she had had smallpox. I am afraid she saw me looking at these marks, and at once told me with great pride that they were made by *moxa*. *Moxa* is a cure much admired by the older generation consisting of a small cone made from herbs which is placed on the skin and then set alight. It burns right down, scorching the flesh and leaving a deep round wound. It is supposed to be good for rheumatism and can also be used on refractory children. Children are not much punished until they are about six. If as a result of this they become even more odious than is usual from such spoiling, they are in primitive parts of Japan brutally treated with *moxa*, which is supposed to drive out an evil spirit which has possessed the child. On the whole we didn't think we wanted someone with such evident faith in the efficacy of *moxa* looking after Sebastian.

Eventually we chose an extremely dignified-looking woman called Nabeta San, and agreed to pay her a wage of $15 a month. For this she would come every morning at seven and not leave until the same time in the evening, and we were considered generous in giving her a whole day off each week. Curiously enough she was one of the few Japanese we met who had been divorced. Her husband, she was continually telling us, had been a man of enormous cruelty, and one could believe it because the provocation required to make anyone willing to undergo the stigma of divorce must be very great, for in the web of society there is no place for a woman who has abandoned her husband. Ruth Benedict in *The Chrysanthemum and the Sword* tells of a girl who had been turned out of the house by her mother-in-law for no more reason than that she did not much like her. The girl's husband was extremely fond of her, but his opinion was of no importance. When she was turned out she was pregnant. Shortly after the child was born the mother-in-law came to the house where she was living and removed the child. The young woman acquiesced in this even though she knew that the mother-in-law had no intention of keeping the baby but was going to give it to foster parents. If it stayed with her it would have no status, whereas with the foster parents it would be completely accepted as a member of a new family.

Nabeta San actually did have two grownup children of her own. She was, to start with, absolutely amazed at our methods of bringing up a child. She would be acutely miserable if we ever reprimanded Sebastian, and could not understand at all how we could bear to leave him alone in a room, nor how we could possibly not go to him when he cried, however many times we explained that he would only cry the more if we were to go and pick him up and carry him around, which is what she wanted us to do.

Children are one of the most attractive aspects of Japan.

They are the only people who have any liberty except perhaps for very old people, who are past enjoying the privilege in any but a tyrannical fashion. To have children is regarded as most important. A childless couple is somehow pitiful, and the woman has to bear a burden of shame. The vanity of the Japanese man is such that his virility must never be called in question, and he heaps the disgrace of not having children upon his wife. The arrival of the first child in any family is therefore a great source of relief to all. The husband is a man in the fullest sense and the woman has her purpose in life. The child itself is consequently a symbol of success for everybody and is treated with appropriate gratitude. When my wife later had a baby in a Japanese hospital she was kept awake all night by the other mothers in the ward chattering ceaselessly to their babies, thanking them for their appearance and promising them a wonderful life in return.

Certainly the life of a Japanese child is, for the first six years, idyllic. No one ever reprimands it, it is never left alone for more than a few instants, it is given whatever it wants, it can stay up until any time, it is cosseted by anybody who comes to the house. For a while, anyhow, children are the most engaging members of the community. They are remarkably pretty and, as everyone is anxious to please them, they are very responsive and happy. It is noticeable that children in Japan talk at a very much earlier age than they do in the West. Often they are prattling away at about one year old; the result, one supposes, of the fact that someone is always talking to them. Boys, it is true, have an even pleasanter life than their sisters, the universal respect for the male being evident at the youngest age. Even their mothers treat little boys with a certain deference, and if there were any situation in which rules of precedence arose, quite small boys would take a place before their mothers. The only rule which they are taught is to bow. Most children are carried about on their mother's back in a sort of hammock, often of embroidered velvet. When the mother meets anyone of her acquaintance she bows herself, and reaching up pushes her child's head down. Children are also house trained at a remarkably early age, but otherwise there are no restrictions.

After a few years something has to be done. It is, of course, the little girls who suffer most from the new regime. Silence is imposed upon them and whereas a little boy may sprawl in his bed, girls are made to sleep with their legs straight out, unfolded, close together. Once the age of freedom is over, at about the time a child goes to school, the new attitude of restriction is enforced with a severity equaled only by the laxness which preceded it. The results are alarming. It is quite a common sight to see a child of about seven lying orange with enragement on the sidewalk of a busy street yelling as if it had been dismembered. The sudden shock of the transition from complete liberty to rigid discipline is one from which I believe no Japanese ever recovers. There is a breaking of the spirit which I think can never be entirely healed. There is a shattering of assurance leaving a scar of timidity which can, in the case of men, only be concealed by a recourse to arrogance. How else can one account for the paralysing nervous tension with which one feels every man one meets to be charged? How else explain the bluff, bullying attitude which collapses with the first breath of opposition? It may, it is true, be only part of the explanation, but certainly it is one part—and a fairly large one. One, too, which appalls you each time you see the stage being set for its re-enactment.

The other person whom we added to our lives while we were in the inn was Yanagawa San. I had asked the Tourist Bureau in Kyoto to find someone to teach me Japanese. Yanagawa arrived one morning with a host of credentials and recommendations to the effect that he was a first-class interpreter, fluent in English and French and accustomed to the ways of foreigners. He was about twenty-six, one of Japan's perpetual students and a perfect example of the imposition of a totally new civilization upon the old one. He came rattling into the room with a sort of nervous clumsiness, which I later realized represented for him an imitation of the atmosphere of breezy bonhomie in which he believed all Westerners lived. He was wearing a pair of blue, stained trousers, shiny in the way that an antique acquires a patina. Above this he had on a sweater, also blue, with the word *Moku* worked in white on the waist. His face was creased with a smiling desire to please until his eyes entirely disappeared into two folds of skin. He wore his hair in a wild brush style, pushed up into the beret he was wearing so that the cap floated on the top of his head. He had surprisingly good teeth for a Japanese, with an enormous mouth, so that one's first impression of him was a great beaming smile full of teeth, apparently directly underneath his strange cap. He bowed four or five times, jerkily and as if ashamed of doing so at all, and then launched into a description of himself.

"I am Moku," he said, pointing to the name embroidered

on his sweater. "All the French people call me that. I am very *apuré*."

He snatched off his beret with one of his jumpy gestures, dropping at the same time a bundle of papers. "All *apuré* people wear a beret," he said. "*Apuré garu*," he said by way of explanation.

It wasn't for a little while that I understood that this meant *après guerre*. This was the term—now abbreviated to *apuré*—which the students used to describe themselves as being intellectual and independent, the opposite of traditional. The beret is their symbol—"my hunting beret," Yanagawa used to call it—for they have an extravagant admiration for anything French. One would see these berets everywhere, especially at such Western entertainments as the opera and the ballet, at which they would keep them on all through the performance. When it became really hot, Yanagawa changed his for a sort of linen golfing cap with a suppressed peak. This was known as "my promenade hat."

We stumbled along in English for a while and then it became plain to me that he was really only at the stage one would expect of someone who had learned a foreign language at school. He told me with mysterious confidence that he was merely rather rusty—"after a little practice I shall be perfect, as I am in French." I tried a little French, and a cryptic flow came from him in which I could distinguish two words: "*surrertut*" and "*puroofate*". However, whatever his shortcomings, I was completely won over by his certainty that he could do the job and the plain fact that he needed it, if only to buy a new pair of pants. Indeed he became the mainstay of our life, and however exasperating I do not think we could have managed, without him, to do half the things we did.

Every morning Yanagawa would come to the inn to give me a few hours' lesson in the language. His English improved very little, with the result that it was a very laborious process, the more so as he had no sort of scheme or plan by which one might learn easily. We merely struggled along together and after a while a certain pattern did become clear. Japanese is not a difficult language to learn badly, but its refinements are extremely complicated, so that after a month or so I was able to manage shopping and traveling without much difficulty. Moreover I learned enough for it to become plain that the Japanese language has a very marked effect on the people themselves. Obviously this is a question of which is cause, which result; but certainly now it is the language which affects the people. There is a basic vagueness about the language which inhibits the speaker from making any too definite a statement. It is almost as misty as the landscape. At the beginning of my lessons, I used to note down during the day various sentences which I had needed and then ask Yanagawa what I should have said to express them. I remember one peculiarly frustrating morning when there had been a tremendous rumpus in the inn the night before. A furious amount of telephoning at about one o'clock had woken us. This was followed by considerable shouting and a great deal of thumping and banging. So on my list of phrases I had written, "What happened last night? Was something wrong?" Yanagawa wriggled about, making the curious grunting noises he produced whenever he was embarrassed. "Well, it can't be all that difficult," I said. "They are two perfectly simple questions." "Ah, yes," he said, "very simple for you." At length he wrote down a very complicated sentence in Japanese which I then read out and asked him if I had pronounced it correctly. "Ah, yes, very good. But we would never say that, of course." He had spent ten minutes preparing these elaborate phrases.

"Well, whatever would you say?" I asked.

"*Yube do shita no*. Last night—how was it?"

"Well, that's all right, I can understand that. But what about the second part of the sentence: 'was something wrong?' "

"Ah, we would never ask that. It would be much too rude, implying that the inn was not a good one."

They always read ten times more into anything than one could possibly expect.

"But what would you say?"

"We would say '*do shita no*'. Just repeat the first question."

When I pressed him, pointing out that he had produced a sentence which seemed to cover exactly what I had wanted to say, he explained that although the words existed, they would sound as strange to a Japanese as an English sentence like "did wrongness occur?" would sound to us.

Similarly, it is possible to say in Japanese, "I am Mr. Watanabe." On the other hand, the usual phrase which somebody uses for introducing himself is "*Watanabe des' ga*." ("I am Mr. Watanabe but...") What does the "but" imply? There is really no satisfactory answer. Perhaps it means "I wish I wasn't," or, "but you will not be interested," or indeed it may be a manifestation of Buddhist evanescence meaning "What does it matter, I could be called anything

else and I won't be here in fifty years anyhow." It seems to
be employed really to avoid the uncomfortable sensation of
making a definite, precise statement. If you go to an inn and
ask, "Are there some rooms?" the reply will often be
"*Arimasu kedo* (there are, however)." This certainly means
that there are rooms, and that you are welcome to take them.
Nevertheless the "however" leaves one with what is supposedly an agreeably indefinite situation. It may be that it is
excessively polite, the however being equal to a little notice
saying NO OBLIGATION TO BUY. Nevertheless, the innkeeper
would be very surprised if having given you this answer you
did not accept the rooms, given that the price was reasonable.

This vagueness permeates the whole language. Tenses are
relatively of very little importance—anyhow, as far as the
future is concerned. It is obviously a little hard to get around
the fact that the past has occurred, but the question of
whether you use the present or the future tenses, inasmuch
as these do relate to our own tenses, is really a matter of the
strength of your intention to do something or of the prob-
ability of something else occurring. There are no relative or
personal pronouns, which makes the construction of some
sentences extremely clumsy. Another confusion for foreigners is that the same word pronounced in exactly the
same way can have as many as eight or ten meanings. To
take at random an example from the dictionary, the word
me can mean eye, sight, meshes of a net, squares, tooth, texture (of cloth), grain (of wood), discrimination, a measure.

The confusion which arises from this astonishing number
of homonyms often makes it very difficult for the Japanese

to understand one another in conversation. It is a perfectly common sight to see a man drawing the pattern of an ideogram on one hand with the forefinger of the other in order to explain what he has just said. It is just possible to say the sentence "The journalist came to his office by train" repeating the word *kisha* three times. The thing is further confused by the fact that many ideograms may be represented by different words which mean the same thing. Thus, the word *okii* and the word *dai* both mean large, and are both represented by the same sign.

The results of all this are very plain to see. At the simplest level, you can never be sure what arrangement you have made. "I would like to come to your party if I can manage it" is probably a refusal. I remember one occasion when we had a friend staying with us and I had arranged for him to be included in a dinner party which was being given for us by a monk. As it happened, our friend had to go away earlier than he had expected, and so we called on the monk to explain that this friend would not be able to come. The conference on the subject was very elaborate, involving a good twenty minutes of polite exchanges, half an hour going around the temple looking at treasures, and a further twenty minutes getting away. Just before we left I asked my friend whether he had really explained to the monk that he wouldn't be there for the dinner and, when he assured me that he had, I asked him once again just to make certain. Needlessly fussy, you might think, but, in the event, when we got to the dinner the following day the monk said, "Where is your friend, is he not coming?" It seemed that the most the friend had said was a polite expression that if anything happened to prevent his coming, which of course was out of the question, he would be most disappointed. The monk being of the Zen sect, and consequently more direct than most of his countrymen, had somehow overlooked the sentence which my friend had thought was a completely adequate apology for his not being able to come.

At a higher level, it seems to me that this imprecision has in fact drawbacks of almost national importance. The Japanese are hampered by a language which prevents them from following a logical train of thought, from developing a concrete theory, even from establishing any true communication with one another or with the outside world. It may be picturesque, attractively inconsequent, it may be encouraging for the pursuit of enlightenment through illogicality and even somewhat enviable to those who are limited by the dictates of reason. But in the modern world it is a disaster. In the same way that kimonos are delightfully pretty to look at but wholly impracticable if you have to catch a commuter's train to get to work, so a language which abhors directness is adequate for a closed civilization more concerned with ritual tea parties than practical affairs, but a positive disadvantage to an overpopulated country which has to compete, for better or worse, with the practical logic of a world concerned with modern industrial production. And that is the world in which Japan now has to live, if it is to survive. It is remarkable that in the face of it Japan has become the most highly developed country in Asia.

By this time we were becoming familiar with Kyoto. Every day we would wander down from the quiet, almost rural peace of our inn over the gorge and through the little shrine and plunge into the town with its whirl of urban sensations so out of key with the almost timeless quality of our Japanese life. The town, as I have said, is hideous. But after a while one discovers beneath the surface of rattling streetcars, hysterical traffic and modern street noises the underlying core of the ancient town, which represents to all Japanese the epitome of their culture, of their historical heritage. It is the city which illustrates most sharply the incredible dichotomy of the country. Nowhere are the old traditions so deeply reverenced, and yet no city so prides itself on being up to date. There are dotted round the city at least fifteen hundred Buddhist temples in which the monks live a life in essence no different from that of their predecessors over the past five hundred years or more. Side by side with them are cinemas, slick offices, and in various quarters the incredible profusion of bars with vivid neon signs and names like Pepe le Moko and Brigitte Bardot, testifying to the imposition of a new way of life. In the same street you will find a little lantern-maker, working in his shop with only his family to help him, pasting colored paper over a framework of bamboo in the way that his ancestors have done for hundreds of years, and next door a huge six-storied department store in which you can buy anything from a ball of string to a $300 crocodile bag, and where you can see copies of the latest fashions from Dior, in which you can even get married. You will see a geisha girl in her kimono, her face elaborately painted and her long hair piled up in the traditional style waiting on the pavement to cross the road, while a multicolored truck with a gigantic mock tube of tooth paste on its roof and a blaring loud-speaker inciting everyone to brush his teeth, goes past.

As you go through the streets you may see a girl carrying a *samisen* on her way to a lesson, and at the same time we used to set our watches by the moment at which a huge carillon on the top of a department store would blare forth the pathetic strains of Dvorak's "New World Symphony." Next door to the *kabuki* theater would be a *pachinko* parlor. These last are most curious phenomena—something like amusement arcades. In them are row upon row of machines, often as many as two hundred in a parlor. The machines are simple. One pays two hundred yen, or about sixty cents, and is given in return one hundred small silver balls. One after another one feeds them into the machine and pulls a handle and the ball spins up to the top of the machine and then falls down, finding its course between a maze of pins. If one is lucky the ball is trapped by the pins and falls into a hole, and in return one wins ten or twenty more little balls. At the end of a session, if one has more balls than one had started with, one can trade them in for a few packets of cigarettes or sweets. It is a monotonous game but apparently it has some fascination for the Japanese. The parlors are never empty in spite of the fact that there must be about a hundred of them in the town, and one may have to wait ten minutes or more before one can find a machine that is free. Old and young, men and women, even schoolboys, all queue up to try their luck at the game. There they stand, motionless and drugged by the flashing and tinkling of the silver balls, hour after hour. It is a strange sight to watch—the solid ranks of people pushing in the balls and flicking the handles hopelessly, endlessly. One hears of men who waste the whole of their income on this game, and the fascination which it exerts on the people is undeniable in face of the fact that there are eight million of these machines in the country.

While one half of the population seems to be losing itself in this bleak escape, the other half is trudging almost as dazedly around the sights of the town. They come in hordes to the famous gardens and temples of the city. At the garden of Ryoanji, with its fifteen stones set carefully haphazard in a bed of regularly raked sand, they stand and stare. Not seeking the deep meaning which Westerners try to impose on this abstraction, but rather absorbing the blank atmosphere of infinity which it creates. In a sense it is not a far cry from the random tumble of the pin balls.

One never manages to sort out these contradictions. One merely becomes so accustomed to them that they no longer seem odd. It is much the same with all the contrasts in Japan. You endeavor to analyze them, but, if you allow them to worry you, you reach a point of frustration in which it is no longer possible to enjoy anything. As in the case of the language, if you come to examine them with a logical eye they merely depress you as being so hopelessly absurd and inefficient, so insulting to the canons of common sense that you despair of Japan's ever being more than a makeshift compromise. Given that you are prepared to be uncritical and unanalytical, then the charm of Kyoto grows imperceptibly with time.

The whole atmosphere of the city is enhanced by its compactness. It was originally laid out in a checkerboard pattern, modeled in a rather too ambitious style on the same plan as a Chinese city of the seventh century. The streets run, almost all of them, directly north and south, east and

Dressed as a woman Fumio San dances in the bar he runs for *Kabuki* actors. All female parts in *Kabuki* are played by men.

Moku Yanagawa, our interpreter.

The Inland Sea, with its mass of minute islands, has been the inspiration for much that is typical of Japanese Art.

Peace Square in Hiroshima. The arch is directly below the exact point where the atom bomb exploded.

Hot spring baths are frequently out of doors. The temperature of this one at Tottori is nearly 120° F.

The village of Obama, with the sulphurous springs steaming at the sea's edge.

The folk museum at Kurashiki is representative of the more adventurous architecture of this district.

Mount Unzen, itself barren and scrubby, is regarded almost as a place of pilgrimage, perhaps because of the view from the summit.

The temple of Saidaiji, illuminated for the festival, was originally founded about 750 A.D.

Anything up to a thousand boys attempt to crush themselves into the Temple.

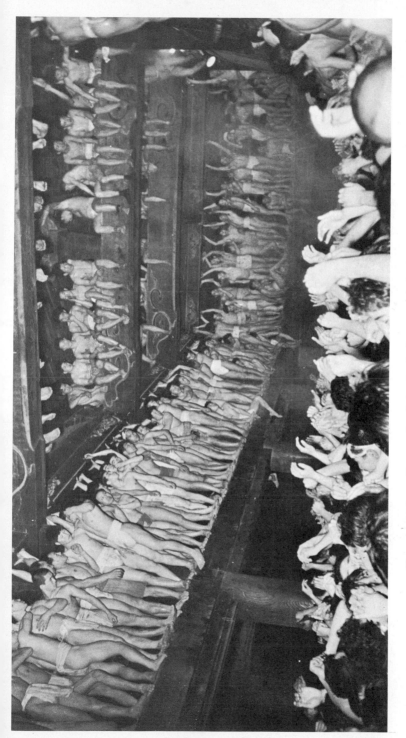

To escape from the crush of the festival many of the boys climb up into the rafters, until others push them down again into the press of bodies.

Osho San, the abbot of Shinjuan Temple.

Shinjuan Temple was founded by Ikkyu a famous Zen master (1394-1481).

ōā San was exceptionally punctili-
s in her manners. Every time we
t the temple she bowed deeply.

The journey down the Hozu rapids.

Ozaki, one of the students, lives in a poor quarter of Osaka.

Inoue, another student, has the lo face associated with woodbl prints of *Kabuki* actors.

Kuma, the village where the seminar was held, is typical of villages all over the country.

west, so as you look down the broader ones you see, as you do in New York City, the sky at the end of the streets. Furthermore, as the town is so small, there are few places from which you cannot see some part of the high ring of mountains which surround Kyoto. Even through the crowded traffic you can drive in on one side of the city and across the depth of it and out into the pure countryside in less than twenty minutes; and to drive from north to south takes little longer. From the bridges over the wide Kamo River in the center of the town it is possible to look up the broad stony bed, often splashed with the bright colors of silks drying in the sunshine after being washed in the water, and to see where the river narrows to the flow of the rushing torrent from the hillsides and in winter to glimpse the snow on the mountains which feed it.

The feeling of the country is never wholly lost within the city. Quite far in are patches which have somehow escaped the spread of buildings. You will find perhaps a quarter of an acre of paddy field with the rice plants growing right up against the houses. Butterflies flutter around the tram stops. The gardens add to this effect. You may step out of the busiest street through an unobtrusive gateway and find yourself totally removed from all urban context by the skill of a Japanese gardener. Each of the fifteen hundred temples has its own garden, be it only the size of the average living room, but more care will have been lavished on it than on a whole park in England, in an endeavor to achieve the same sensation of space. Each section of the city has its own distinctive quality. In the northwest is the weaving quarter where, if you walk down any little side street away from the traffic, you can hear the clacking of the looms turning out brocades and silks. The northeast side, near the river, is where the larger businesses produce the long strips of material which you see by the riverside or hanging like vast streamers from frameworks forty feet in height. A little to the south of this is the university quarter with its mass of tiny coffeeshops and seedy bookstalls. In the center is the shopping and tourist district, varying from large mock-Georgian banks, which cluster around one intersection, to little unpaved streets with curio and antique shops and special places where they make large Japanese clothes for foreigners. In another quarter live the papermakers; in another the potters. And one whole district is given over to the curious twilight world of the geishas. The effect of this division of the city into little sections is to increase the feeling of its being a small town, for it is possible to live a complete life without ever stirring to any other part of the town. Each section is like a little village with its own pursuits, its own grandees, its own village idiot.

There is no real need to step out of one world into another. In each little part there is a market, and everywhere a plethora of little shops, often no bigger than a few square feet, so that within a few hundred yards of one another there will be two or three fish shops, two paper shops, three flower shops and a myriad places to buy cakes and sweetmeats. So compact are these sections that sometimes you will meet people who, in spite of the general passion for travel, will never have ventured out of an area smaller than the size of Greenwich Village.

We were naturally drawn to the small section near the

river, where one could find the best antique dealers, print sellers and old-fashioned brocade shops. Shopping was one of the greatest delights in these little places run by one man and his family. There was never any pressure on one to buy. Instead one was assured of a pleasant welcome and agreeable light conversation. We would go into a brocade shop and squat down on the floor, cups of tea would be brought and the proprietor would sit beside us, and once he had got to know us would call in to someone to bring out the things which he thought of special interest. The question of being known was all-important. The prices were completely adjustable and once they had learned I was English, not American, that already knocked off 20 per cent. That I was a writer was worth about 5 per cent; that I was living in the Japanese quarter knocked off a bit more. Four or five visits reduced matters still further, and then one would start to bargain. I remember going in one day to a little shop and buying a string of fairy lights for the Christmas tree. I asked the price and was told what seemed to be a perfectly reasonable sum, and promptly agreed to it. Whereupon the shopkeeper, whom I had never seen before, took my money and gave me too much change, saying "twenty per cent off," for absolutely no reason that I could gather. Such is the nature of prices. Yet somehow there is none of the pleasure—or anyhow very seldom—of driving bargains that you have in the Mediterranean. In Japan you feel that the man needs too desperately to sell whatever it is, and also you feel that the complications of the web of obligation may even induce him to sell it at a price lower than is reasonable, or even economical for him. The only comfortable course is to know the right price for each thing, and settle for that.

In these little shops like the brocade one we would learn a good deal about the customs of the country. The proprietor would show us some special coat which used to be worn by *samurai* in the old days, or a beautiful embroidered square bag, like a cushion with the feathers taken out. This was a formal cover in which wedding presents are given. On one side might be a picture of a cockerel with a long tail in front of a shrine and on the other, woven into the material, a family crest or device, for after the wedding these covers are given back with a small parcel of dried fish to alleviate the obligation placed on the bride's family in accepting the wedding present. The proprietor, while showing us something of this sort, might discourse about weddings, or about *samurai*, for about half an hour, and he would not seem disappointed if in the end we bought nothing. Perhaps he was, but I think not, for the passion which all Japanese have for explaining their national customs—a part of their great self-consciousness—makes up for the lack of business. They are also endlessly courteous.

Near this narrow district of antique shops was the main geisha quarter, known as the Gion. Like so many of the other districts it is almost entirely devoted to one activity, and is virtually self-supporting. There are the living quarters of the geishas, the tea houses where they meet their clients, the *samisen* makers who produce their instruments for them, the cooking shops which have meals ready to send around to the tea houses at a moment's notice, the dressmakers who make the elaborate kimonos for the geishas. The whole area is centered around the unique institution of the geishas.

People who know nothing about it think that geishas are prostitutes. Those who claim to be "in the know" will tell you that they are nothing of the sort. The cynics are without information, but far nearer to the truth. The geisha is a prostitute, but at her highest level the most respectable of her profession in the world—that is to say, the most expensive. Originally the geisha girls were dancers who could be hired for a special occasion, and this is still true. But in addition to this they have rather more important functions. It is decided at quite an early age that a girl shall be a geisha. Either she lives in the Gion quarter or in another nearby quarter called the Ponto-cho, and is therefore caught up in the way of life. Or she may be sold by her parents for anything from about ninety to three hundred dollars to a geisha house.

The training starts at the age of about five or six, and nowadays there are special schools in these quarters so that the young girls can anyhow appear to be complying with the new compulsory education laws. At the age of about fourteen or fifteen the girls graduate to being *maiko*, or apprentice geishas. They will go out and entertain, by dancing and singing and conversation at dinner parties. The geisha house is run by a sort of madame, who was herself probably a geisha. She pays for their education and their expensive clothes and generally sees to their welfare. The outlay is great. Part of it is paid back out of these dinner parties, which are perfectly respectable, also remarkably tedious. The usual pattern is that the men get rather drunk, and the geishas spur them on with provocative chatter until the moment of danger occurs. Then they leap up and dance, usually some nostalgic Japanese folk tale and then, when everyone has simmered down, they sit again and the whole process is repeated. For foreigners they will usually try to produce some Western music which they have learned from the radio, and as conversation is usually difficult, they resort to games. These are on the worst parlor-trick level—an endless procession of patacake and balancing coins. The conversation, if one can understand it, is seldom an improvement on this, being composed of rather childish forms of innuendo and coy references to love. Many people protest that if one could really be proficient in the language then one might get more out of it—the jokes might be funnier—but I do not believe it. And on the occasions when I have been with Japanese at a geisha party and they had been rolling about merrily, when pressed the joke always seems to have been some sickly pun on beans and vaginas, which happen to be homonyms. There is, anyhow for me, something distasteful about hiring a woman by the hour to entertain you in conversation. It is somehow almost worse than a prostitute, for at least she doesn't have to pretend to enjoy it. There is something specially disagreeable in the fact of someone breaking off almost in the middle of a joke, however feeble, and saying, "Time is up, I must go now."

Although they are paid at the rate of fifteen dollars an hour, this is not sufficient to reimburse the madame for her capital investment, so there comes the other side of the life of a geisha. She is sold to a *danna,* or master, for several thousand dollars, as his exclusive mistress. The *danna* in

modern times is usually a businessman, for it is only on an
expense account that the luxury of a geisha can be afforded.
Her duties to the master will be the obvious ones of a mistress and the job of entertaining at business dinners. It is
unthinkable to have a wife present at such an occasion because everybody is bound to respect your wife except you.
Therefore if there is to be someone then it must be a person
before whom one can conduct what passes for an argument
in Japan. It is part of the skill of a geisha that she shall be able
to smooth the path of negotiation between her master and
his guests. Apart from this, a geisha who has been sold to a
danna continues to earn money by entertaining in the
ordinary way, as she did when she was a *maiko*. But by this
time the madame has been paid off and these earnings are
her own. So the geisha enjoys an independence denied to any
other class of woman in Japan. A married woman is completely bound up in her husband and children, and an unmarried one who goes out to work will still live with her family and give the larger proportion of her wages to them. It is
rare for a geisha to marry, although it sometimes happens
that if her master is widowed she will consider becoming his
second wife in the true sense rather than the sense in which
the phrase has been used about her during the wife's lifetime. Their usual ambition, however, is either to become a
madame themselves or to open a little bar or wine shop and
thus preserve their independence.

All this applies to the highest class of geishas. There are
other girls who have much the same training but who are
more simply prostitutes. These can be met in much the same
way and owe an allegiance to a madame. They are usually

ones for whom it has not been possible to find a prosperous
master. Sometimes they belong not quite so strictly as their
seniors to a lower executive in a firm, or they may be even
more generally available. It is quite a normal custom if you
are asked to a dinner by a businessman for there to be geishas
of this sort present. I remember a friend of mine telling me
that he and a colleague went to dinner with someone with
whom they had some dealings and two geishas waited on
them and sang and danced. At the end of dinner the host ex-
cused himself and they were surprised that after half an hour
he did not reappear. The geishas appeared to get restless,
and it turned out that the host's disappearance was the
height of delicacy and politeness. They were now expected
to go to bed with the geishas. The girls were most put out
when my friend and his colleague were reluctant to take advantage of this arrangement. They begged to be allowed
merely to sleep in the same bed with them, as they felt first
that they would lose face, and secondly their code of honor
dictated that they must do something in return for the
money they had already been paid. It is not only foreigners
who are caught out by misunderstandings of this sort. An
editor of one of the leading Japanese newspapers told me
that he always used to enjoy coming to Kyoto because, after
a good party the night before, the four regular geishas who
used to entertain him and his friends over dinner also used
to turn up at the station to wave good-by. He thought this
most touching until one day the manager of the branch
of the newspaper in Kyoto asked him most deferentially
whether it was absolutely necessary for him to have four
geishas to see him off at the station, because the office ex-

pense account was heavily strained by the sixty dollars which was charged for this agreeable service on each of his visits. Would not just two be sufficient, the manager suggested miserably. Quite incidentally, this was one of the few occasions on which I ever head a Japanese tell a story which made himself appear in a foolish light.

Such, then, are geishas. A brittle, doll-like product of the closed civilization of Japan. They are pretty, certainly, but in a sexless, formalized way. Until they are older, so exact is their training that it is hard to distinguish one from another. They are somehow pathetic in their artificial uniformity. Their clothes are one of the most picturesque uniforms in the world, but they are designed to make them as unindividual as a troop of guardsmen. Their hair, their dead-white make-up with red rings around the eyes, make them appear flat and characterless. The only time I ever saw one caught off guard was in the *kabuki* theater, when a geisha turned around and realized that I had noticed her picking her ear with her spectacles. She looked most embarrassed, and during an interval made a great performance of eating a juicy peach without one drop of it falling on her clothes or marring her lipstick. I found it almost more comic to watch the unnatural gesture of popping each little piece with two fingers right on the back of her tongue and then closing her lips in a tiny O to keep the juice in, than I had to see this little overdelicate figure give way to a natural impulse.

In sharp contrast to the rarefied quarter of the geishas are the barely mentioned districts of the *Buraku-min,* or untouchables. It is hard even to get Japanese people to admit that they exist—and officially they no longer do. Yet as you

walk about Kyoto, or any other large town in Japan, you
come across forlorn areas of a few blocks in each direction
in which you are suddenly aware of a change of atmosphere.
It is not just a question of poverty, for heaven knows this is
universal enough. It is more that one is conscious of a blank
dejection mingled with a suspicious resentment at one's being
there. There is, too, less pride in the streets. There is more
litter, which is unexpectedly absent in other parts of the
town. Hardly anyone seems to bother to throw water down
on the road to lay the dust. The children are coarser and less
restricted, and even call out insults as you pass. There are
more people hanging about, plainly out of work. They are
quite easily recognizable, these untouchable districts.

The origin of the outcasts who inhabit them is hard to
establish, or at any rate would be if you relied on the information given you by casual acquaintances. If you even get
as far as making a Japanese admit that they exist, which they
will when you have told them three times that you are in-
quiring about something of which you have positive proof,
they will probably tell you that they are Koreans or descendants of prisoners. When later I was teaching a class of students, only one of them would really talk about the matter
freely. Here are some notes which he wrote out for me, not
necessarily accurate or even tenable:

Buraku-min

They are not of foreign race, nor are they the descendants of prisoners from other countries. At the beginning
of its reign, the Tokugawa Government set up, under
military, agricultural, artisan and mercantile classes, a

still lower class—*buraku-min,* for mere political reasons.

As early as the Medieval Ages there were people called *kawaramono* or *Sanjo-no-tami,* who made a profession of handicrafts such as tanning, dyeing, smithery or gardening, and of entertainments, such as *Noh* or other dramatic performances.

Now, they were compelled to go out of town and make a settlement of their own on the outskirts, as it was necessary for the Tokugawa Government to flatter farmers into thinking that they were not the most miserable, far better than some people else, so that the Government might exploit them to the full extreme, "without letting them live nor die"; which was a motto for its policy toward farmers.

The same intention can also be seen in the social discrimination established by the Government: military, agricultural, artisan and mercantile classes. Notice that the agricultural class stands second only to the military class which naturally stands highest as it was the world of *samurai*: while in reality, however, farmers were leading the most wretched life. One might argue for other reasons why they put farmers into a high social standing, but it is only obvious that they aimed at flattering farmers, giving only nominal privileges to them; "Don't look up, but look down and live" was the attitude to life enforced on people. And *buraku-min* is a victim of this policy of the Tokugawa Government's. Absolutely innocent, ancestors of *buraku-min* were driven out of town, living a hardly human life to serve as a set-off to farmers. Masterless *samurais* joined them (for, remember, it was soon after civil wars) and farmers who, unable to pay heavy taxes, secretly left their home and land by night, also joined them. It was a highest crime to stop farming and leave the land where you belonged, and once you left it, you could not go elsewhere.

This social discrimination was most strongly enforced from Temmei to Meiji Eras (1781-1868), and more than 80 per cent of six thousand still-existing outcast communities (*buraku*) were only forced into being during this period. More and more reasons were invented and added to, as time went on. The social discrimination was indeed indispensable for the military class, for without it they should have fallen long before from their high estate, and only with that privilege they could manage to reign over artisan and mercantile classes that had already had a strong economic power, while they had lost it. Or rather, they had none from the first.

This discrimination was abolished, it is true, when it was declared in the 4th of Meiji, 1871, that people of all four classes (including, of course, *buraku-min*) are equal in social standing as well as occupation, but the discrimination still exists and comes to the front whenever the problem of marriage, finding employment or anything like that occurs.

In fact, these people's lot is now almost worse than it has ever been. Originally, various trades were set aside for them, as the notes above show, but the "abolition" of the class merely means that other people can now indulge in these trades without disgrace, while the *eta* or *buraku-min* are eased out of their jobs and find it almost as hard as ever to get any other kind of employment. The dossiers and letters of recommendation and general gossip which are consulted before anyone is offered a job in Japan, make it virtually impossible for anyone to conceal his origin. It is even difficult for the women to become prostitutes.

A brothel—or a bar or restaurant, for brothels were officially closed in 1958—is the most usual place for a prostitute to carry on her trade, and a brothel keeper will be as searching as any other employer in her inquiries when recruiting new staff. If a girl turns out to be an *eta* she will stand no chance. The lot of the *eta* has little possibility of being improved. The only people who might take an interest in them are the few of their numbers who have managed to break through the barriers, but these are the least likely people to do anything about them, for their chief preoccupation is to conceal their own origin. The whole situation is one of the finest examples of the national characteristic of pretending that anything unpleasant does not exist. The newspapers occasionally carry an article on the subject, but such articles usually reveal little, and anyone who reads them ignores them as being journalistic sensationalism. I remember that when we finally got a house I asked my cook, who lived very close to an *eta* district, about these people. "Oh, you mean the Koreans," she said. "We pay no attention to them." Had we offered to employ some of them, I feel the cook would then have paid some attention. She would have left.

Our stay in the inn came to rather an abrupt conclusion. Ishida, the master, having little to do, occupied a great deal of his time in busying himself about other people's affairs.

I think that he also felt himself to be a slightly ridiculous figure, which is an almost unbearable situation for a Japanese. The consequence was that he stormed around the house finding fault with everyone except for Yaoko, who was the general peacemaker. For some reason he particularly took umbrage against Nabeta San, Sebastian's nurse. He used to come to me full of tales about her iniquities which, on close examination, he could never substantiate. One day I heard him ranting even more abusively than usual, and went to the kitchen and found him yelling at her, and she in tears. It seemed that he had caught her combing her hair in the kitchen, which he pronounced to be a very unhygienic act. It didn't seem to me that the general standard of cleanliness in the house warranted such scruples, so with a great deal of palaver we left within an hour, forming a rather comical procession as we walked down the little path over the bridge and through the shrine, carrying the chair and table which we had introduced into the inn, and a mass of clothes which we had not had time to pack. The whole staff of the inn came down to where we kept the car, and we drove away leaving behind us a little semicircle of six bowing figures who had quickly put on their kimonos in honor of the occasion and were weeping at the disgrace to the inn. When I went back there about a month later, to see if some lost letters had been sent there by mistake, I found that the whole staff had changed. Even Yaoko was gone.

CHAPTER SIX

THE HOUSE

Our need to find a house was therefore greater than ever. We had during our stay in the inn become rather lazy about hunting for one, preferring to spend our time learning about Kyoto. After following a few abortive trails we were lucky.

The northeast corner of Kyoto has one small, rather prosperous quarter. The houses are, many of them, built in Western style. The streets are unpaved and uncluttered and each house has a garden of some size. To reach it you go along a pleasant road lined on either side with trees and just beyond lies pure countryside rising steeply to Mount Hiei— a famous mountain, dotted with temples, once the strongholds of marauding monks.

Our house was in this quarter. It was a Western-style house of which we could have the ground floor, consisting of two occidental rooms and two Oriental ones. There was also a Japanese bath but unbelievably a Western lavatory. The house belonged to the widow of a naturalist called Kazama. I like to think that this accounted for the wire screens over the windows, which during the summer kept out the invasion of whirring insects, for someone told me that Mr. Kazama

111

had put up these invaluable screens not to keep the insects out but to keep in the ones that he was studying.

Mrs. Kazama was one of the most delightful Japanese that I met in the whole time we were there. Her father had been a *samurai* who owed his allegiance to one of the Shogun's staff at the time when the Emperor Meiji took over the power of the country and dismissed the last of the Tokugawa Shoguns. Mrs. Kazama's father had sat outside the Shogun's palace for three days and nights without food or sleep in protest against his acquiescence in the Emperor's plan. His protest being useless, he quickly set about learning a trade, as did most of the *samurai*, who were abolished as a class after the restoration. Like many of them, he was very successful in building up a large silk business, so that before the war the Kazama family were extremely rich and influential. In the fashion of the day they built themselves a Western house. Indeed they built more than one, for each time one of their children got married they seemed to put up a new one.

So we lived in the largest, with a German couple on the floor above us, and next door Mrs. Kazama lived in another. When I say Western house I should perhaps explain that the Japanese idea of how Westerners live was not then very clear. The result was that ours was something of a cross between a suburban house on a by-pass and a railway observation car. There was a mass of fancy brickwork and a number of diamond-paned windows and, under the windows of the sitting room, a sort of cocktail-bar seat, built in and upholstered in pink. The wallpaper was of a design which I remember having in my bedroom at school. The overhead lamp was a wooden monstrosity of a chandelier. But the

comfort of being able to sit up after crouching on the floor
for a month and the unbelievable kindness of Mrs. Kazama
made up for all aesthetic shortcomings.

Mrs. Kazama was a women of seventy-five and a member
of a class which had suffered a considerable upheaval. The
samurai were strictly a leisured class. They had had no wars
to fight for hundreds of years. Even after they went into
business they managed to maintain a dilettante approach
rather in the way some English people do today. But the
Pacific war brought this situation to an abrupt end. Mrs.
Kazama suffered the same sort of privations as her counter-
part in England, only to a much greater degree. The country
gentry with whom she might be equated managed throughout the war in spite of having to do their housework, in spite
of rationing, in spite of the Labor Government, to maintain
—anyhow among themselves—a sort of myth that they were
somehow superior. In Japan this is simply not so. I never
heard anybody under the age of sixty bandy about phrases
like "good family." Although the product of the strictest hier-
archical system ever devised, they are curiously lacking class-
consciousness in the English sense of the term. People's
position, while it is still one of the most important factors in
Japanese social intercourse, is no longer based exclusively
on birth. Even the grandest Japanese never seems to question the people he meets in your house. It may be that I was
deceived by the politeness, but even allowing for that I still
found them the least snobbish people I had ever met.

Mrs. Kazama, who had a strong nostalgia for the old regime, was genuinely interested in the poor working-class
students who used to come and see me. And for all that she

would correct me for using an honorific when I was talking
to Nabeta San about her daughter; she never gave any signs
of believing that any rights were due to her by virtue of
being a *samurai*'s child. Unlike her English equivalent she
did her own housework, or anyhow a great deal of it, without
complaint, but it is true that the position of a servant in any
household has always been much more that of a member of
the family than it is in Europe, and housework is not despised. The war had reduced her to great poverty. It was not
just a question of a rise in prices, but in order to survive,
being someone who could not work, she was obliged to sell
all the clothes and beautiful brocade sashes which were the
trousseau of any Japanese woman of her class. She used to
show me photographs of her children's weddings shortly
before the war. The bride's family would provide for their
daughter almost enough clothes to last her the whole of her
life. I remember in one photograph a pile of *tabi*—the boot-
shaped sock with a division for the big toe which is worn
with a kimono. There were something like seventy-five pairs
—twenty-five for winter, twenty-five for summer, and
twenty-five for spring and autumn. The brocade *obis* could
cost as much as three hundred dollars each, and each daughter had, too, a large diamond solitaire ring. There was no
hope of selling their jewelry, for the Government com-
mandeered all jewels, promising to pay the owners when
victory was won. It was interesting that practically no one
kept anything back. Mrs. Kazama, telling me about this, said,
"We gave all our jewels gladly to the Emperor. We would
not have dreamed of keeping anything for ourselves, how-

ever great its sentimental value." And today it is a very rare sight to see any woman with more than a wedding ring.

Mrs. Kazama held no resentment that all her sacrifices were in vain. She had the Japanese acceptance of fate, of the changing order of things, and of one's powerlessness against them. The furthest she would ever go was in deploring the lack of manners of young people in the universal way of all persons of her generation in whatever country. She bore the Americans even less animosity than did most of her countrymen. They had been billeted in her house—the one which we now took—and she accepted them exactly for what they were, either polite and helpful or inconsiderate. The strongest thing I ever heard her say against them was a mild attack on their taste, prompted by the day she came in and found them about to paint her treasured English wallpaper a blank white.

She was of an age to be able to speak her mind, and so she was easier to talk to than most of the other people I met. Her upbringing in a Canadian mission school may have had something to do with the lucidity with which she was able to express herself, unlike most of her countrymen. But I think it was also due to the freedom of spirit which may have come only with widowhood, but which is in fact present in all Japanese women if one can only persuade them to release it. Whereas it is unusual to find it—even the germ of it—in Japanese men.

Housekeeping was something of a revelation to us. Our rent was sixty-five dollars a month and we had two servants to whom we paid twenty dollars each a month. We ate well enough but by no means lavishly, although it must be admitted that we did buy a number of things which were imported and consequently expensive. Our bills amounted to forty-five dollars a week for food, electricity and general housekeeping expenses. We lived therefore at a rate of two hundred and eighty dollars a month, which is to say more than either of our servants earned in a year.

One can imagine, then, at what kind of level the average person in Japan must live. A fair wage for a white-collar worker is often as little as forty-five dollars a month. I believe that the Prime Minister earns less than we were spending on housekeeping. A university professor never gets a living wage, but has to eke out his salary with translations.

The average person sees meat only about ten times a year and eats very often only rice for several consecutive meals. It is hardly a cause for wonder that the people are thin, that they fall asleep as soon as they sit down in a tram, that a sad apathy marks their faces and their movements.

CHAPTER SEVEN

THE SCHOOLTEACHERS

Food at seminars is always a subject of importance. We think you will find the food, on the whole, is wholesome, tasty and sufficient in quantity to satisfy you most of the time."

These were hardly very encouraging words with which to accompany an invitation to go to a seminar for schoolteachers in a remote village on Shikoku, the smallest of the four main islands. Nevertheless I went. The seminar was organized by the English faculty of the university in the largest town on the island. It was held for the benefit of high-school teachers from all over Shikoku.

The man in charge was called Shigeo Imamura, a young teacher at the university who had been trained in the teaching of English at Michigan University. He had been born in the United States, where his parents had emigrated. However, it seems that shortly before the war they had decided for one reason or another to return to Japan, and Imamura, who was ten, had completed his schooling in his homeland at the time when Japanese imperialism was at its strongest. The effect on him as a boy was dramatic. Everything which

117

one supposes he had been taught in America was wiped out by the all-pervading influence of the militarist doctrine.

Soon after he left school Imamura volunteered for the Air Force and, at the very end of the war, underwent training as a *kamikaze,* suicide pilot. He was totally dedicated to the Imperial regime and it was only by a fortunate chance that he survived. The day came when he was to go on his first—and necessarily last—mission. He dressed himself in his best uniform and attended the final ritualistic ceremony for the pilots who were to fly out that day to destroy themselves in the act of destroying the enemy. He drank the prescribed cup of *sake* and was about to take off on his death flight when orders came through canceling all *kamikaze* operations. It was a few days before the end of the war and the final defeat of the regime for which he was prepared to make a total sacrifice.

Meeting him one would have no inkling of his wild, fanatic past. He was a gentle man, with a soft and pliant face which seemed to be fired only with a boyish enthusiasm. There was about him, though, a certain air of authority, almost perhaps the assurance of a mystic. It may be that this was the only thing that remained from the curious certainty which he must have possessed in his youth. Otherwise, except for a love of military precision, he had given over everything to his interest in teaching English.

I arrived with a companion rather late at night, a day earlier than we were really expected. Imamura was putting the finishing touches to a complicated loudspeaker system which he was rigging up all over the school buildings in which we were to live and teach. He was the first Japanese

I had met who could speak absolutely fluent and idiomatic English. He showed us to a room which was normally a classroom. The desks and chairs had been bundled into a corner, and about half a dozen *tatami* mats laid on the floor in one half of the room. There were the usual quilts to sleep on, and rather unexpectedly a couple of blankets.

When we woke in the morning we found that we were at the fringe of a small village set in one of the most attractive valleys I had seen in Japan. We had climbed up the night before about three thousand feet and now we were high up in the mountains in a world very different from the cultivated atmosphere of Kyoto to which I had become so accustomed. It was delightful on that first July morning to walk down the village street and encounter a new sense of friendliness, so unlike the more formal attitude of people on the mainland. Nearly any Japanese from Tokyo will advise you against going to Shikoku. "Such a backward place," they will say, "such barbarous people, who have no manners." But it was, frankly, a relief to find a people less constrained than those closer to the center of civilization. In the end, I came to realize that almost any place against which I was particularly warned by my more educated friends was almost certain to be extremely sympathetic. The villagers of Kuma may not have had those last refinements of pruned politeness, but they were certainly extremely welcoming. Everyone called out to us some sort of greeting as we searched for the restaurant where Imamura had told us we could get breakfast. We found it—a tiny little place known to the teachers at the seminar as "The Green Pea," because of their custom of giving one a saucer full of peas with almost everything one ordered—even whisky and soda.

We went through the door and were immediately confronted with a small arched bridge spanning a stream full of live eels which ran through the room. Beyond it was a cobbled floor set with tables and upturned wine casks for seats. To the right was a bar and, further over, the kitchen. Even in this out-of-the-way place a great deal of trouble had been taken to make it look attractive. There were rocks dotted in appropriate places, giving it the atmosphere of a grotto, and a number of plants growing quite naturally indoors. A girl waited on us, bringing the customary bean soup to which I had now got quite used, a few pickled gherkins and seaweed and, of course, bowls of rice. She was a friendly girl who took an assiduous interest in one's affairs. "Are you English or American?" she said, and when I said I was English she became brighter than ever, and said, "Then you must be a gentleman." It is a strange myth, this, which can survive so persistently even in the large cities as well as in this tiny valley which probably fewer than twenty English people had ever visited.

We could have wandered about in the village for hours, chatting with the shopkeepers, who didn't seem to want to sell anything particularly, and whose only concern was to show one the painted wooden dolls which were traditionally carved in the valley. But the schoolteachers were due to arrive at any minute, and Imamura was determined to have a military parade at the earliest possible moment.

We were all assembled in the large lecture hall and given our instructions. The object of the seminar was to drum into the teachers a certain amount of idiomatic usage. This was to be done according to a system developed in Michigan University by which a class full of people would repeat again and again the same common English phrase, substituting on each occasion a different word at the key point of the phrase. The instructors were expected also to give occasional individual tuition to teachers with particular problems, and to conduct classes of free discussion and, at some time, to give a lecture. The whole job was not arduous, and Imamura's rigidly arranged timetable was so organized that one was by no means overworked. Nevertheless, these ten days of teaching gave me a greater insight into the tangled problems of the Japanese character than almost any other experience.

The very fact that the seminar was held at all was a triumph over one of the curious prejudices of the Japanese academic world. The ability to speak a language well is rated very low. Whether this is a result or a cause of the fact that the Japanese are almost unbelievably bad linguists is a little hard to determine. But on the whole, I am inclined to think it is an effect rather than a cause, because the question of face is necessarily involved, and it seems to me more likely that it is because they are so bad at learning to speak languages that they have come to despise the achievement as being a rather vulgar one. The older members of the Faculty of English at Ehime University are constantly trying to undermine Imamura's efforts, to teach his students that they are wasting their time listening to him and that they should merely concentrate on learning how to read and write the language. It is partly due to the fact that there is an extremely enlightened governor of the province who gives Imamura great encouragement and assistance that the seminars are held at all. Nearly everywhere else in Japan, English is taught as though it were a dead language, exactly in the same way that we learn Latin and Greek. The result, naturally, is that although a boy may have studied the language for fifteen years, he is quite unable to carry on even the simplest conversation.

This became rapidly apparent when we came in contact with the schoolteachers. On that first day they were set an examination, mostly in the form of dictation, and the results were not encouraging. Nevertheless, the method of teaching was extremely simple. In my first class I merely had to say a sentence such as "this is the kind of pencil I like," and then the pupils would repeat it after me. I would then say "hat," and they would say "this is the kind of hat I like." This formula would be repeated over and over again using different sentences with the object of getting the rhythm of English into their ears.

The first thing I found was that it was useless to single out one teacher and ask him to repeat the sentence on his own. The result was always total silence. The vast majority of them were incapable of repeating even a sentence of twelve syllables without a mistake. Obviously I would notice that one or two of them were better than the others, so I would ask them a question, or tell them to repeat something, and a stony silence would ensue. I could not understand this frustrating blankness until it was explained to me by one of the other instructors, who had done this kind of thing before, that even if the man knew the answer to the question he would be reluctant to give it. I gathered that it was a matter of face. The brighter teacher might well be a junior teacher. He could not therefore show up his senior colleagues by knowing the answer to a question which was beyond them. In addition, they hated having attention drawn to them— being singled out before the others. Even if it was the most senior teacher he would rather appear simply to be a member of the group. The group had an entity of its own. Either they all knew the answer, or none of them did. It was the simplest form of the amalgamation of the two great influences in Japan, the system of hierarchy and the unimportance of the individual.

I learned quite quickly to overcome these difficulties by curious devices, such as saying, "You all know the answer, let Hamada San be your spokesman." This worked, after a few days anyhow, when I had got their confidence. But occasionally the whole thing would become too much for me, and when one particularly irritating man would hang his head and simply not reply I would forget the Japanese courtesies and reprimand him. The results were astonishing. The man would either apply to be put into a lower class or quite simply go into a decline, and have to rush off after the class for treatment in the sick bay. There were of course smart alecks amongst them, ones who didn't seem to care about the group spirit and were bent on becoming a sort of teacher's pet. But I discovered that usually if one inquired into their backgrounds they turned out to come from one of the little islands inhabited by only a few hundred people or to have some slightly different history from the usual teacher.

They were all intensely serious and had an almost touching faith in anything one told them. I came to have a nightmarish fear that if one said that Shakespeare was now entirely discredited in England and that nobody read him any longer they would have gone away and torn up their copies of his plays. Partly as a result of their methods of learning a language, they had a passionate interest in grammar and knew more names for parts of speech than I had ever dreamed existed. Moreover they seemed to have tried to formulate a rule to cover every possible juxtaposition of words. Often when simple euphony dictated a difference between two phrases they would have invented some enormously complex rule of grammar to explain it away.

It was noticeable that they usually asked one the same questions that everybody else asks: how long have you been in Japan, what are your impressions of our country, how do you like Japanese women—do you not think they are beautiful, what do you think of Japanese customs, do you like Japanese theater? Apart from inquiries as to how the educational system of England was organized, they always put questions about their own country. I noticed that whenever we had a free discussion in class they wanted only to talk about the way things were done in Japan.

In my class one morning was a slightly sad little figure called Miss Uno. She was not pretty, but on the other hand she was more responsive and intelligent than most of the rest of the class, who were nearly all men. In free discussion the subject of how Japanese women were changing was brought up. They all claimed that Japanese women were becoming modern and emancipated and quite different from their mothers. I asked them whether they would prefer to be married to a modern girl or one who was more inclined to follow the traditional meekness. All but a few of them said they would prefer modern girls. "How many of you are married?" I asked. Four put up their hands. "To modern girls, or traditional ones?" "Oh, very modern," they all said. "How often do you take your wives out?" "Oh, quite often." "You, Ashida San, how often?" "On her birthday—once a year." "And you, Hamada San?" "About once a year also. Sometimes twice." One of them said he took his wife out once a week, and the others all looked at him in amazement.

Later that night, when I was talking to a group of them before they went to bed, Miss Uno came up and said, "I did not speak in the class this morning because I was shy. But now I will tell you—I would like to be married very much, and I should like to be a modern girl who went out with her husband very often. But it can't be." "Why not?" "I am very ugly," she said, "and if I were married and my husband took me out everyone would stare and feel sorry for my husband for having to be out with such an ugly wife. So if I ever do get married I shall be a traditional wife and stay at home because I could not bring that disgrace upon my husband."

Two of the instructors carried out an experiment which I would never have attempted, which was to get their two classes to conduct a debate. They chose what seemed to me to be a subject in extremely bad taste, even had Japan been a country which had a vaguely parallel sense of humor to that of the Western world. The subject was, "As it does not now look as if Japan will ever become one of the leading

countries of the world, would it be better for her to join
the British Commonwealth or to become another of the
States of America?"

Certainly they intended this as a frivolous argument, but
in fact the teachers debated it in absolute seriousness. There
was one boy who dissented from either suggestion, and produced a theory, perfectly sincerely held, which reflects something of the astounding mixture of humility and arrogance
which goes to make up the Japanese character. With great
portentousness he stood up in the middle of the debate and
said, "It is quite true that Fate has denied Japan the possibility of becoming the great nation which she should be. I
have therefore a solution which will make the best of her
unique talents. There is no doubt that the Japanese are the
greatest people on earth. They should therefore be dissemi-
nated over the whole world, in every country, like the Jews.
In a short time they would rise to the top in each country and
become the natural governors. They could then link with
their own people in every other country and govern the
whole world in peace and amity. There would be no more
war, and the population problem of Japan would be solved."
My colleagues did not attempt a second debate.

One of the most typically Japanese events during the
whole seminar was the excursion which we took to what was
considered a great beauty spot. The expedition was arranged
with enormous precision by Imamura. Two buses were
ordered to convey everybody to Omogo, which was supposed to be the most beautiful gorge on the island. I rather
shabbily preferred to go in my own car, and took with me
one of the instructors. I asked some of the teachers if they

would like to come as well, but they all said they preferred the bus, not wishing to be singled out from the group. The drive to Omogo was quite spectacular. The road wound along beside a river, seeking its way through the high mountains. Every time we turned a corner I thought we must at last have reached the place, for at almost every turning there was a perfect position for a picnic. But it did not matter how attractive the places were that we passed—Omogo was one of the three most beautiful places in Shikoku, and Omogo was where the seminar excursion always went. It was unthinkable that anywhere else would do.

The drive took about two and a half hours over the dusty, bumpy, unpaved roads, but when we at last reached our destination there was no doubt that it was extremely beautiful.

The buses stopped at what appeared to be a deserted quarry. From there we went on foot up a steep, stony roadway, and on going through a tunnel we came upon what can only be described as a glen. Steep banks covered with maple trees rose on either side and at the foot of them a stream rippled over a stony bed. As one walked down farther, the banks steepened into cliffs and we found ourselves in a narrow gorge. Here the stream ran faster, rushing over the pure white stone which was the floor of the gorge and cascading into blue-green pools that were deep and clear.

At the most beautiful point there was a flat recess in the cliffs with a snack bar and a small hotel plastered with notices advertising noodles and fried fish. Here we all scrambled down to the stream and tested the ice-cold water to see if we could bathe. Very few of the teachers ventured in, but most of the foreign instructors thought it worth trying and suffered miserably from the ferocious horseflies which attacked us as soon as we exposed any part of ourselves above the water.

I noticed that in each of the clear turquoise pools there was an unexpected glinting at the bottom. For the moment I attributed it to some unusual rock formation—perhaps mica in the limestone. However, this was not the case. After we had bathed we all ate the food which Imamura had provided. It consisted of sandwiches wrapped in shiny mauve paper and a can of mandarin orange juice. After being nearly two hours in this place we set off back to Kuma. As I turned to look once more at the gorge I could see one hundred and three pieces of mauve paper scattered over the banks and stones, and in the depths of the pools a hundred and three bright shining tins. They were all amazed to see me still carrying mine, and offered to throw them away for me, but I made a great show of trudging back to the car clutching on to them. We then drove back two and a half hours over the dusty roads satisfied that at least we had been to see one of the three most beautiful places on the island.

There is, it seems to me, an almost painful duty imposed upon the Japanese to go to the right place. No matter whether it is a shrine or a mountain, a temple or a gorge, before it is worth going to see a seal of approval must have been set upon it. I never heard one Japanese person say to me, "I will take you to a little place I know of where no one ever goes. We can have it to ourselves." Instead, in busloads and trainloads they flock year after year to the same hallowed places which they share with a million others.

This reverence for the recognized place does not admit

of any critical approach. Anywhere that is supposed to be beautiful is beautiful. Mount Fuji must be viewed from the right place. There are standard places from which to view the moon, ones which you must go to even if you are trampled underfoot. The cherry blossoms and maple trees are virtually ignored in some valleys, whereas it is impossible to get a glimpse of them in others because of the crowds. The important thing is to go to the right place. Once you get there it doesn't matter what you do—you need not bother to preserve its beauty for anyone else. What matters is that you have been there, and when somebody mentions the hills at Takao you can moan out the words, *"Aah, so des'ne?"* The result is that the most famous parks of cherry blossom are totally ruined by the ankle-deep litter, by the drinks and the hideous huts selling postcards and food. The only comfort is that you can find delightful groves of cherries, unexpectedly beautiful temples, and have them all to yourself while the Japanese are sucking up their traditional, specified, culture.

Perhaps the most agreeable part of the seminar were the evenings off which we spent in the hotel in the village. This was a pleasant little inn in the village street on the same side as "The Green Pea." Once again the stream ran through the house. There was another arched bridge curving over the running water and mossed stones. Beyond this was a good-sized room in which all of the instructors met in the evenings. We sat on the floor around two low tables drinking beer and *sake* and going off in turns to have a bath, for the bathing arrangements in the school, while perfectly adequate, were not particularly agreeable as one had to share them with one hundred teachers.

We were waited on hand and foot by the three girls of the inn, who were of an infinite silliness that was somehow rather engaging at the end of a day's work. They were more forthcoming and direct than the young girls on the mainland and were forever flinging their arms around us, tickling us and making improper jokes and comments. It was difficult to judge how far they would have gone, but one had the feeling that they had the freer and easier habits of the Japan of fifty years ago, before Western disapproval changed the moral tone of the country. They were extremely jolly and did not seem to mind sitting for hours on end in the midst of a conversation carried on in a language of which they did not know one word, requiring only an occasional amorous glance and enjoying, night after night, the same jokes about how tall we were and how much we were able to drink.

In this rather convivial atmosphere Imamura and the other Japanese instructors seemed to relax more with foreigners than was usual. The conversation seemed always to be about Japan. Like everyone else, they were much more interested in learning our views about their country than in learning anything about ours and they seemed much more ready with genuine criticism than most of their compatriots. I was quite used to people saying, "Our roads are bad, I am so sorry for it," or, "Japanese men are not so good to the women as you are." These sort of remarks were clichés, to be heard everywhere, and were thrown out with little real belief in their truth, and perhaps merely to have them contradicted. In any case, most people looked rather crestfallen when one agreed with them. On the other hand, Imamura and his friends were genuinely trying to analyze the differences between the Eastern and the Western approach to things. He, as I have said, spoke perfect English, and there were two of his colleagues who were reasonably fluent.

One evening we were discussing the contradiction of both the extraordinary politeness of the Japanese people at home and their ingrained community spirit, as opposed to their atrocious manners as soon as they got outside their houses. It is one of the most noticeable things in Japan. A crowd is almost a free-for-all. You can do anything, and no one will complain. I remember once a small boy, who wanted to see a procession, biting me in the leg in order to attract attention to the fact that he thought he should be in front of me. I gave him a mildly savage kick, at which his parents roared with laughter. But it is more serious than this. Two events stand out in my mind. First, soon after I arrived, a young girl on a railway platform was precipitated, in the usual violent struggle to get near the door of an approaching train, straight on to the line underneath the engine. The other occasion was on a boat which was making a comparatively short journey on the Inland Sea when a sudden storm blew up. The passengers panicked on the deck, rushing from side to side as each new wave beat against the ship until in their frenzy they pushed two unfortunate passengers overboard. The ship then put back to port, which it reached in perfect safety. This kind of disaster is perfectly commonplace—as common in fact as it is unnecessary.

Imamura explained that the Japanese code of conduct was laid down at a time when there were no crowds—no need for them, for everyone lived a compact life in his own community. A friend once said to me, "Often I see in Western films an old man walking by himself through a public park. This would never happen in Japan. He would be in his own garden." There was no equivalent in the old days of the English pub. The Japanese man would spend his evenings at home. So it was, Imamura said, that when completely new demands were made upon the Japanese by the imposition of a mechanized culture, they who had lived always by a strict code of politeness found they had no rules to cover the new situation, and for want of rules behaved in a completely barbarous fashion.

Kawakani, one of the teachers, said that one could be misled by this into believing that all Japanese actions in public were rude, whereas in fact some of them are only rude by Western standards and, as it happened, very polite by Japanese standards. "I can think," I said to him, "of someone in a wheel chair who is often pushed about Kyoto by his wife. Sometimes when they come to a very steep step it is difficult for his wife to get the chair up it. There may be half a dozen young Japanese men standing about, but none of them ever offers to help. Can you call that polite?" "Certainly," said Kawakani. "It is a perfect example of what I say. To you it may seem rude that they do not help. But to us it is excellent manners to ignore your friend. First of all, to go and help him would be to draw attention to his disability, and secondly it would place him under an unbearable obligation to the helpers."

"That seems to me a monstrous distortion of common sense."

"Of course it is, but that is what I am talking about. You will sit there and judge us by your values, and they simply do not apply."

"Do you think then that it is perfectly all right if someone is involved in an accident not to go and help them? Why is it that if one happens to be present when there is a car smash that people all stand around gaping and it is almost impossible to get them to help even if somebody is quite badly hurt?"

Kawakani's face at this assumed that mask which one usually comes up against much sooner in an argument with a Japanese person. It is a kind of withdrawal, and when it appears one realizes that one is going to get no further.

"Japanese people," he said, "perhaps react slower than Westerners to any situation in the sense that their imaginations are stronger, and therefore they are more shocked by something of that sort."

"You cannot honestly believe that."

Imamura laughed at this, and made what was perhaps one of the most significant remarks I ever heard in explanation of the Japanese character.

"When I am in an American mood I would agree with you. And when I am in a Japanese mood I would agree with Kawakani. On different occasions I would give you different answers to the same questions. It depends perhaps on which language I am thinking in."

I must say for Kawakani that it was not for long that he preserved his withdrawal. He too agreed with Imamura that he was able to see both sides of the question. It does not mean that he was torn between two opinions, for it is an innate skill of the Japanese that they can quite happily hold two totally conflicting views at the same time. A belief in Shintoism and Buddhism is a perfect example. Underneath, I believe, there is a conflict of which they are barely aware. Certainly with these men it was partly a question of language. Their own language did not compel them to think anything out logically, but they were familiar with English and with the need that English imposes on one for logicality. Certainly Kawakani's next remark revealed something of this.

"We believe essentially in the thing of the moment. That is our only absolute. Before the war, for instance, we believed in the slogan 'southeast Asia co-prosperity sphere.' After the defeat of Japan we have exchanged that for the slogan 'liberty and peace.' It may be that we could exchange it again quite quickly for another one."

"Are you able," I asked Imamura, "to throw off all the teaching and indoctrination which led you to become a *kamikaze* pilot? Do you, for example, still believe the Japanese are the chosen race of the gods and are superior to any other race?"

"That is one of the questions to which I would answer No in an American mood and Yes in a Japanese one. If I am in an American mood and thinking in English I believe that all men are equal. But if I am in a Japanese mood among only Japanese people then I can still believe, half and half, that we are superior to white people, and know with absolute certainty that we are infinitely superior to black ones."

I am grateful to these teachers at what is after all a small university for anyhow preserving a degree of their American mood and being franker than anybody else, for I think it is their opinions, freely expressed, which gave me some understanding of the problems which confront the Japanese in endeavoring to cope with the alien culture which they have had to accept. Their attitude was a grateful contrast from that of the friend I mentioned before, who produced the typically allegorical illustration of the old man walking in the park alone, which served only to show up the differences rather than the potential meeting-ground between East and West. His attitude on this subject was much more typical, with the resigned pride of the Japanese, who would rather conceal the problems beneath the romantic façade. I remember his saying to me, "The Japanese have two faces. It is quite impossible for them to talk to foreigners as they talk among themselves, so you will find it very hard to get at the facts. The reason for this is that they have made no sacrifice. In Europe everything has been achieved by bloodshed and revolutions. In Japan they have been bloodless. After years of peaceful acceptance of the regime we opened ourselves up. We had been quite satisfied with the rickshaw; we felt no need to improve. It was only to compete with you that we needed cars. So as we made no sacrifice we felt a need to make ourselves mysterious. Nothing was forced on us, so we did not want to abandon our old ways—merely to hide them from the world."

It may have been an accurate assessment of the reasoning behind the two faces of the East, but it was a blind acceptance of the situation which I feel neither Imamura nor Kawakani would ever subscribe to.

The ending of the seminar was a typically sentimental

Japanese performance. On the slighter levels they seem to manage to get more involved than most people of other nations. There was no party, exactly, but on the last evening the teachers and the instructors gave little skits for the benefit of each other. I myself took part in what we imagined to be a take-off of a cross between a *kabuki* and a *Noh* play. It was one of the few times that I saw the Japanese laugh happily at themselves, though afterward one or two of the teachers did come up and beg me to believe that in reality their two traditional theaters were more serious than we had made them out to be. The teachers themselves rather surprised me by singing amidst great bursts of laughter a very martial song, the words of which can be translated as follows:

If we go to the sea we shall find a watery grave,
If we go to the mountains we shall find a grassy grave,
For the sake of our Emperor we shall certainly die,
Nor shall we ever return.

It turned out that this was a favorite song during the war, and they were a little dubious as to how we would receive it.

After the charades and singing the teachers came up, one by one, and went through the most affecting farewells. One boy told me that he had listened to a lecture I had given on life in England with particular interest because he had written to the Queen to congratulate her at the time of the coronation and had received what he termed "a very polite reply." He was sure, he said, that we must love the Queen much more than they did their Emperor, because she had never had to make the renunciation which the Emperor had made at the end of the war. They all promised to write, and managed to give the appearance of being desolated at the ending of our connection. It was one of the hardest things to distinguish real emotion from false, for as it happens the Japanese have an infinite capacity for loyalty to friends, as I was to find out when I finally left the country.

On the last morning the teachers all did much the same test as they had done on the day they arrived. It was slightly ironical that many of them did far worse in this final examination than they had done in the initial one, but Imamura told me that this was always the case and that it was nothing to be depressed about.

CHAPTER EIGHT

NOTES ON JOURNEYS

AT dinner during the first week of our stay in Japan a young Englishman who was at the British Embassy as a language student warned me about the hazards of traveling on one's own. He was thoroughly depressing, particularly when he heard that I had brought a car. "Oh, you will never manage by yourselves," he said. "The roads here are simply appalling and the maps are all inaccurate and if you ask the way people will deliberately misinform you." He went on to explain that one could not possibly stay in any Japanese inn unless it were listed in the official guide of the Tourist Bureau, and that it was positively dangerous in the remoter sections and that one was quite likely to be set upon, robbed and even killed.

Luckily I had a distinct feeling about the attitude of the majority of the Embassy officials. It was something to do, perhaps, with the fact that they all lived in a walled compound, in houses built in a mock-Georgian style. For the most part they seemed completely divorced from the reality of Tokyo, cut off and self-sufficient. They met only a very few selected Japanese who make up a sort of diplomatic pet shop. There are about sixty of them—the Japanese—who toil

138

around from one diplomatic function to another, as if specially appointed to the task of providing local color for the foreigners.

As it turned out, Japan is the most delightful country to travel in. Certainly the roads are atrocious, but one rapidly becomes accustomed to that and adjusts one's arrangements accordingly. The maps that one can buy are not very good, but they are perfectly adequate and only once do I remember having to go fifty miles out of the way because the map, issued incidentally by the Tourist Bureau, promised a good wide road where in fact there was none. The people, far from obstructing one, are wonderfully helpful, and often they will leap into the car in order to make sure that you reach your destination even though it may take them far out of their way.

The only mild hazard about asking directions is that in the country no one will believe that a white person is going to be able to speak even one word of Japanese. Often I used to lean out of the car to ask the way from some old man and before I had even uttered a sound his face would cloud with incomprehension. One might ask quite simply for a three-syllabled town like Kazumi. There cannot be many ways of pronouncing this, but no matter on which syllable one placed the emphasis the old man would continue to shake his head and declare that he could not understand. I eventually learned a satisfactory technique. It was no good merely barking out the name of a town, even in faultless Japanese. The important thing was to convince his ear that it was going to hear a sound which was familiar. The Japanese in conversation always go through a great preliminary of rumblings and grunts and respectful noises. So my method was to lean out of the car and prefix my question with the equivalent of, "Well, er, I mean to say, this is how it is ... however ... er, here we all are, er ..."—in fact, carry on just like Bertie Wooster before coming out with my question. The result was very satisfactory and, once I had learned it, I found I could get anywhere.

The trains are very efficient and nearly all electrified. They run very well to time and are perfectly comfortable although nearly always crowded, as the Japanese love any excuse to travel and rush miles to the wedding of a friend, to honor the anniversary of an ancestor's death, or even to attend an exhibition at the opposite end of the country.

The particular delight of traveling was the inns. Not by any means the large Westernized versions which were listed in the Tourist Bureau Guide, but the simple ordinary inn which was to be found in any village with more than about one thousand inhabitants. It was the greatest comfort to know as one drove aimlessly about that, at the end of the day, you could be sure of finding somewhere agreeable to stay wherever you happened to be. The standard did not vary very much from one end of the country to the other, or from the urban to the rural districts. Wherever one was one could be certain of finding three things: a hot bath, a passable meal and a flat bed. And really one could not ask for much more. I would far rather make an unplanned journey in Japan than I would in England.

In whichever inn one chose, there would be the bustle of girls to meet one, giggling and simpering, but nevertheless determined to please. The bath water would be ready at any time after four, and on coming out of one's bath one would be brought a meal of raw fish and fried fish and perhaps a chicken leg in one's own room—nobody eats in a dining room—and then, when one had eaten, the quilts would be brought out from the cupboard and laid on the floor. And once one had learned the trick of using the seating cushions as pillows, rather than the viciously hard little bolsters provided, one could be sure of sleeping comfortably.

The standard varied a little in the finer points of cleanliness, for it is a myth that the Japanese are a clean people about the house. They go around with little dusters, flicking the dirt from one ledge to another, but they seldom busy themselves with cleaning in the way that we understand it, and it never occurs to them to do anything above eye level— which is to say above one's shoulder level. In a little mountain village there might be in the hallway an open fire with a kettle suspended over it, or an elaborate contraption weighted with a large carved or metal fish which acted as a weight so that the height of the kettle could be adjusted over the flames. The smoke would rise into the room and disappear out of the eaves of the roof. And here the matting of the roof might be worn thin and the bath be little bigger than a large barrel. But the principle was the same as it was in a larger inn at a hot-spring town where the *yukata* they gave one after one's bath would be made of real silk and the bath itself might be as big as a swimming pool, the matting a gleaming new straw color and the sliding doors covered with a fancy paper. In all of them one was sure of pleasant friendliness and much the same edible food, and nowhere did one feel a knobbly bed.

We enjoyed traveling almost more than any other aspect of our stay, and the following pages are notes drawn from my diary of those journeys.

• • •

Late in the evening we turned off the main road and branched down a valley leading to the coast at Ako. It was a perfectly formed valley, almost too regular to be real. In its flat bottom the paddy fields stretched from side to side in neat rows of squares, curving up the hillsides a little at each end, giving the whole valley the appearance of a carefully made boat. There were very few houses, and the June sun was large and round, on the verge of sinking behind the hills. Throughout the long day of driving, the land had been bleached almost colorless by the harsh light, but now as the sun prepared to disappear, the fields and the hillsides shone for a while, vivid green, and then slowly as the lambent flush of evening crept over them they seemed to glow with a rich yellow. Our valley joined another almost at right angles to it and we drove beside a wide, still river until we came to the town of Ako, where the water spread broadly out into the sea.

Ako itself was a dull town with only the rough remnants of a *daimyo's* castle, surrounded by a broad moat filled with the pink and white flowers of the lotus, to give it an interest. We pushed on through the town up a winding coast road until we found ourselves in a small village which might well have been on the Italian Riviera. There was a mass of inns and a piazza with cages full of monkeys and deer and, around the edge, chattering cafés. There was a great parade of sightseers, each group wearing the distinctive *yukata* or summer kimono, provided by the inn in which they were staying, marked with the special device of the hotel. We had lighted unawares on a popular tourist resort, with the unfortunate result that there was no room at any of the inns, for it was Saturday night. After trying them all we drove on hoping to come to a less popular village.

The road climbed and dipped, about 300 feet above the sea. At length we saw down on our right a modern building we thought might possibly be an inn. The steep road to it was only half-made and we thought that we would never get the car down there so we went on until we were suddenly checked by a landslide which had completely blocked the road. We went back to the precipitous half-made driveway and nervously turned down it, inching our way carefully and expecting any minute to topple over the side. It was, as we had thought, an inn, recently built. Martha went in to inquire if they had any rooms. She came out again and said yes, they had, followed by a gnomelike grinning man. As soon as he saw the rest of us he darted back into the inn and re-emerged with the proprietor, who said there had been a mistake. There were no rooms. Why, then, we asked, had the first man said there were some? He couldn't account for that, but there were still no rooms. By this time we despaired of driving back up the perilous slope, for it was now quite dark, so we asked if he could give us dinner, and whether we might sleep on the beach. Rather reluctantly he agreed.

The inn was built in a cross between Japanese and Spanish architecture, so they set a table before us in a three-sided patio, the fourth side of which was open to the sea. In spite of the fact that the place could only have been open for a matter of weeks there was a large clientele of businessmen, presumably from the industrial towns a little farther up the coast. While we were eating our dinner, or as much of it as we could save from the wild invasion of little crabs which scurried at amazing speed up our legs and on to the table, there was a sudden disturbance and a family of three people and about four children arrived and asked for rooms. The proprietor beamed at them and said yes, of course. Whereupon we made a good deal of fuss, but the owner merely said that they had booked, which in fact they hadn't, as we could gather from their conversation. However, it seemed more important that the children should have somewhere to sleep than that we should, and anyway we would certainly be worsted in any argument.

I felt rather annoyed as we set off with a number of blankets and prepared to sleep on the beach. It was an ugly discovery when we found that what we had taken in the half-light and several hundred feet above to be a lovely sandy beach was really composed of large hard pebbles. On the other hand the water was wonderful, and in the darkness we stripped off all our clothes and plunged into the sea, splashing about for a long time in the water, which glowed and swirled with a rich phosphorescence. When we got out we lit on the beach a large bonfire of driftwood to dry and warm ourselves. At the sight of this there was a great cry from a mass of boys who were also preparing to sleep farther along the beach under an open-sided tent. They came toward us, piled up our party to enormous proportions and settled down to talk. They told us that they lived in Ako and came out to this beach every Saturday night during the good weather in order to get away from the crowding of their homes. This however didn't prevent them from sleeping, about fifteen in number, under a canopy not more than twenty feet square. They said they had never seen foreigners on the beach before and were determined to make the best of it, however many polite hints we gave about the long drive we had had. They constantly scampered off to get more wood for the fire, sang songs around it and managed to consume all the food which we had been saving for our breakfast. They plied us with questions, including inquiries as to our impressions of Japan, and sat with us for well over an hour, begging us to come back and join them on the beach any Saturday night. In the end, when we finally told them they must allow us to go to sleep, they fully made up for having deprived us of so much of the night's rest by dashing back to their canopy and producing for us quantities of coconut matting and blankets to sleep on, which was probably the only reason we got any sleep at all on the knobbly beach.

．　．　．

We bathed today in a place which agreed precisely with my preconceived picture of the Inland Sea. We had been driving for some time up and down over the mountains which divide each bay from the next. It was hot and dusty and we were depressed at lunchtime by the sight of a strange quarried place which had somehow the forlorn feeling of Spain. There were bare hillocks of sun-scorched earth and, behind, barren stone works. To the left was a row of derelict huts and alongside, stuck into the ground at improbable angles, were fifty or more tattered paper umbrellas. In the scant shade that these afforded, workmen were lying about taking a siesta, as crumpled and as dusty as the land they lay on. They were a pathetic sight.

Just after passing them we came unexpectedly to the sea-shore again. The sea was brilliant, and clearer even than the Mediterranean. Sprinkled all over it were minute islands, rising sharp and green from the blue sea. Any that were big enough to have even two acres of flat land were inhabited and worked upon. Small boats busied to and fro between the islands and the shore. We drove on for some time along the coastline and, where the main road turned to the land once more, we branched off to try and find a beach to bathe on. We were by this time quite snobbishly particular about where we bathed, and kept on refusing places which one would have leaped at in Europe.

At length we found one with a little sandy cove and a promontory jutting out toward the islands. We rushed into the water, which was warm and refreshing at the same time. I longed for some underwater goggles, for all around me were brightly colored fish and bizarre trailing seaweeds. Martha refused to come in because she said there was too much vegetation in the water. I struck out around the promontory, laughed at by a group of small children who were paddling near the edge. The farther out I went the more they shrieked. I lay on my back in the water, splashing idly and wondering what the children found so funny. Suddenly I felt against my foot a nasty spongy mass. I shot away with a vigorous backstroke, but each time I moved once again I pushed against the unpleasant object which I could not see.

The children were by now howling with merriment. At last I got away from whatever it was and looked up to find that I had swum into a mass of jellyfish. They were Portuguese men-of-war, and for some extraordinary reason I had not been stung, rather, I fancy, to the disappointment of the children, who were looking forward to the shrieks they were expecting me to let forth. After that we got quickly into the car and drove back to the village where the main road branched off.

Somehow or other we got lost in the village and found ourselves in a confusion of back streets. At length on turning one corner our back wheels sank into the ditch which ran along the side of the road. Simultaneously our battery expired. This was the cause of great enjoyment to everyone in the neighborhood. The men came and plied us with questions as to where we had come from and where we were going, as to what was our nationality and what were our impressions of Japan. It was by this time rather late, and we didn't feel in the mood for frivolous exchanges. As soon as we had made this plain everyone buckled to and with a great show of ingenuity levered the car out of the ditch with long planks. They then pushed the car for a good quarter of a mile as fast as they could shove it until it started again. None of them would take anything in return for his trouble. It was a typical day's journey.

. . .

We drove to Hiroshima at about nine in the evening. Someone had told us that the Jesuit monks ran a hostel for travelers, so we thought we would try and see if they would put us

up. I wanted to meet them as they had been much involved
in the work of helping victims of the atom bomb. We found
the cathedral and knocked on the door of a Western-looking
house close by. It was answered by a German Jesuit, a surprising red-headed figure in a world of dark hair. He told us
that there was no hostel, but that he would find out from his
maid the name of a suitable place for us to stay. After a few
moments he came out again and said that he knew a place
which could be thoroughly recommended and that his maid
would take us there. He would have come himself, he said,
but he had to attend some convention in Tokyo and was
catching a train in a few minutes. We drove with the mail
until we came to a street which seemed to be filled with inns.
It was surprisingly wide for a Japanese street although dingy
in appearance, the houses being of the usual wooden design,
all shapes and sizes, meeting one another at awkward angles.
We could dimly see that the wood had not yet become entirely gray, but still retained some of the brown color of
newer wood. We realized then that the whole street must
have been demolished by the bomb.

The greeting at the inn was quite warm but slightly
puzzled; and the puzzlement seemed to increase when we
said we would come back in a few minutes with our suit-
cases. There was a hideous jumble, because after going back
to where we left the car and fetching the baggage we
couldn't remember which of the many doorways was our inn.
In fact we got quite far into entirely new negotiations with
another inn before the proprietor of the first came and
hustled us out and took us back to the right one. Once inside,

there was an interminable delay while we sat on the high entrance step waiting to be shown to our room.

"Is it ready yet?"

"No, but it will be in a few minutes. We are just getting it straightened out."

This is an inconceivable situation in a Japanese inn, where there is never anything to be straightened out. But the proprietor persisted in it and we could only wait. There seemed to be considerable voyaging up and down the stairs and to the bathroom, and indeed in and out of the front door. Couples would come in, men would leave, young girls would go to the bath with such astonishing regularity that at last the truth dawned on us. The Jesuit monks had sent us to a brothel. However it was very late, and there was nothing for it but to stay there. At last our room became free, and we went to it, feeling ourselves to be the object of some interest to the inmates.

The room was at the end of a passage, and for economy three of us were sharing it, Martha and myself and another man. Opposite us, in a room with the door ajar, was a rather plain girl, surprisingly on a Western bed, who thought this arrangement quite inequitable. It was absurd, she pointed out, for Martha to have two men. What sort of girl was she, anyhow? Would not everyone be happier if one of us were to go and share her room? Eventually she accepted the situation and turned out to be very friendly, and we spent an extremely comfortable night in a room for the price of about a dollar each, including our dinner and breakfast.

In the morning we set out to explore the town. Hiroshima has quite a different feeling from any other city in Japan. It may be that one's own knowledge of what took place there influences even one's reaction to its appearance, but I do not think so, for Nagasaki does not produce the same sensations. This again may be because Nagasaki was protected in some degree by the hills which divide one part of the town from another. In any case, there really is in Hiroshima a strong sense of difference. The streets are wider, which makes their jumble of Japanese town architecture even more pronounced and accentuates its ugliness. The fact that all the houses are new and their wood unseasoned, gives them an air of even greater impermanence than is usual. In a place where town planning has run wild, where great broad avenues have been laid, the lowness of the buildings makes ridiculous the grandeur of the design.

To the foreigner Hiroshima can represent only one thing. Whereas Nagasaki has a long history as being the only trading post permitted to Europeans for some three hundred years, Hiroshima has nothing—except that it was the first place that man tried out the greatest destructive force that he had ever created. Until one has been there, one can have no conception of the vastness of power unleashed in one single instant. It is not the shadows on the wall, of which you can see photographs; it is not the twisted bottles, squeezed by heat and blasted into unimaginable shapes; it is not the clothes, burned black on one side and still perfect on the other; it is not these which amaze. It is the size of the bomb. It is the fact that you can stand at the point where the bomb fell and know that in whichever direction you may walk, it will take you twenty minutes to reach a house that was stand-

ing in 1945. The sheer area of the destruction, the totality of
its power, is the element that haunts one.

The monuments on the site where the bomb actually exploded are suitable in their simplicity. The actual center is
a rather uninteresting-looking arch beneath which lies the
roll of the dead. It is not more than ten feet in height. To the
south of it is a gutted ruin of a building which was once a
town hall. To the north is a simple modern concrete building, raised on high stilts. The concrete is left rough—there is
no embellishment. It is the museum, devoted to relics and
photographs illustrating the terrors of the bomb. Certainly it
is gruesome and shocking, for it is meant to be just that. But
at no point does it appeal unfairly to the emotions. It is an
honest record of bare truth.

We spent the morning going around the museum, letting
the horror of the bombing seep into us until, in a strangely
definite way, it became important to try and understand the
full effects which that momentary flash thirteen years before
had had on the population of Hiroshima. Somehow the force
of the drama came across the years in such a way that I felt
absorbed by it and wanted to know all that it is possible to
gather from the grim relics, both inanimate and human.

I went first to the cathedral, which was built by the Jesuits
in the ruins of the town. It is a large, peacefully bare church
with simple arches in smooth concrete and has for decoration only one mosaic, over the altar. The striking point of
interest about the cathedral is that on its roof is not only a
cross but also a phoenix—the emblem of Buddhism. It represents a realistic touch of shared misery, for several of the
priests of the Jesuit mission were there on the day of the

bombing. Many died and the others worked on through their suffering. It is disillusioning to think that the placing of this phoenix has been a source of argument between the missionaries and the Vatican.

After going around the church, I went to try and see one of the priests whose courageous activities on the days following the disaster were written about by John Hersey. I could not see him because he had been taken off to a hospital in Tokyo, gravely ill, still suffering from the effects of radiation. I set off instead to go to the Japanese hospital for atom-bomb casualties.

It was a light, cheerful modern building, run entirely by Japanese and built on the site of a hospital which stood there in 1945. I found the director, Dr. Fumio Shigeto, was a simple, forthright man who had none of the aggrieved cant which I had half expected to find among the Japanese doctors. There was no reproach, merely a plain statement of fact and an honest account of the problems with which he had to deal. The question which interested me was that of genetic effects. Before he took me around the hospital, Dr. Shigeto said, "We know so little. The atom bomb has produced no new disease. All the people you will see might have got their illness in the ordinary course of events. As for children, I cannot say. My feeling is that they will be affected. These things we do know—the rate for leukemia is ten times higher here than in an ordinary town—more people suffer from cataracts of the eye. Of other things we are less certain. Cancer seems to be more common, and on the whole people here die younger. But that is all I can say. You must see for yourself."

The hospital had eighty beds, always filled. About sixty to

seventy outpatients were treated daily. The first thing that struck me as I went around was the general lack of despair. There were about six or seven patients to each room, and each room was decorated as if for Christmas, hung with paper crowns and streamers which were supposed to bring good luck. There was a great lassitude, which goes naturally with diseases like leukemia, but at the sight of a visitor most of the patients cheered up and managed to go through the usual formalities of greeting. Three patients in particular struck me. First, Waichi Akutagawa, a sixty-four-year-old bank clerk. He had spread a thin rush mat over his bed and was sitting on it cross-legged as if he were on a *tatami* floor.

"I was only 400 meters from the bomb when it fell, protected by a wall. Until a year ago I used to go regularly to the American Atom Bomb Casualty Commission, but at that time they told me I was clear of all disease. But then, nine months later, I came to this hospital with leukemia. In two months I was out again, and in two months more I was back again. I shall soon be out once more."

When we left the ward Dr. Shigeto told me that Akutagawa could live only a few weeks.

Tomiko Ichikawa is a housewife. She was in a room on her own. Through the paper streamers a long pipe wound down to her arm dripping antibiotics from a bottle into her veins. With her free arm she pulled out a wallet from beneath her bedclothes.

"I was one-point-two kilometers from the bomb," she said.

It is a matter for great pride to all the victims how far they were from what is called the epicenter.

"But look at this picture of my son. He won first prize in our baby contest." And she wept. She wept, I felt, with pride, and with relief that her children were safe from the fate which she could not escape. And yet I wondered when I saw Kazuko Ishi.

She was a bright, gentle child of about thirteen, with all the carefree charm of little Japanese girls. She romped up and down the corridor of the hospital, teasing her grandmother who was begging her to go back to bed. As a tiny baby Kazuko had been 1.4 kilometers from the epicenter. She had suffered nothing until about three months ago, when her liver became affected.

"You see," her old grandmother said, "we will never know when we are safe."

It seems difficult to know at this stage what the effects of the bomb will be on children. Those that were being carried in their mothers' wombs at the time of the bomb were definitely endangered. Many of them were born sickly and weak and many of them have died since. But it seems too early to tell what the effects may be on those children born much later of parents who suffered a large dose of radiation.

I next saw Dr. S. Tabuchi, a gaunt, pigeon-chested gynecologist at Hiroshima University. His special research is in genetics. This man held out even less hope than Dr. Shigeto.

"Besides the acknowledged diseases of leukemia, anemia and cataracts I believe that the bomb caused cancer and shortened many lives among those not perceptibly affected. And I believe that the victim's children will suffer from cancer and their lives will be shortened."

But Dr. Tabuchi too was cautious.

"I can prove nothing," he said. And what figures he had were inconclusive. "It is too soon even now to be sure," he added, "but I believe these things."

I went last to the American Atom Bomb Casualty Commission. Even in the short time that I had been making inquiries I had come up against a natural resentment against the American Commission. I found the director, Dr. T. Darling, much on the defensive.

"You will have heard," he said, "that we whitewash the effects of the bomb, and that we keep our findings secret. And the Japanese will have said that we should give treatment instead of just doing research, and that we dismiss as nonsense cases which the papers describe as victims of radiation sickness."

I said that I had been warned of all these things.

Dr. Darling was a large, burly American of a kind that is recognizable to us as being totally sincere. When he told me his findings I was as convinced of his sincerity quite as much as I had been persuaded by Shigeto and Tabuchi.

"These are the facts," he said. "We do not give treatment because we regard that as interfering, and we do not wish to set ourselves up in competition with the Japanese doctors. We do not whitewash. We have stated that we find a great increase of leukemia among atom-bomb survivors. The same thing applies to cataracts. It may be true also of cancer."

The difficulties of research are prodigious. Two people, five yards apart, may have received quite different quantities of radiation, and different people have different reactions to the same amount.

"We do not keep anything secret," he said. "Our trouble

is to get sufficient concrete evidence. We do not dismiss as nonsense any serious facts, but when the Japanese newspapers make a fuss about a horse dying at the age of seventeen and claim that it is an atom-bomb victim thirteen years after the bomb, our patience is a little stretched."

On the subject of definite symptoms among the children of survivors Dr. Darling was more convincing than Tabuchi.

"We have examined," he said, "some eighty thousand children, and we have found nothing. Some are deformed, some die early, some are diseased. But the proportion of these is no higher than in any other group of children."

Dr. Darling said that the ordinary people of Hiroshima, as opposed to the newspapers and some of the Japanese doctors, showed a touching forgiveness and faith toward the Americans.

"The mere fact that we have been able to examine eighty thousand children is proof that nearly double that number of parents have been prepared to go to considerable trouble for the sake of the community and in order to help us."

In addition to parents, many young people come to Dr. Darling's Commission for advice, for they are afraid to get married. He advises them that they have nothing to fear, but it is advice which he gives with a certainty diluted—or if you prefer, bolstered—by faith. For like everyone else, his conclusion was a cautious one.

"We do not know what will happen to the next generation. We know that there is a certain amount of radiation which will cause a man to have defective children. It is my personal philosophic hope that it is the same amount as that which kills a man."

The fact remains that no one may ever know the true effects of the bomb, for the population of Hiroshima has changed by more than 50 per cent since the atom bomb was dropped. Many of the survivors moved away to other parts of the country, where it is not known that they were victims, for it is a serious threat to their livelihood. A salesman in a shop told me, "I was one-point-five kilometers away from the bomb behind a wall. For two years I never felt ill, but suddenly I had a dizzy spell, and now once every few months I faint for no reason."

I tried to persuade him to go to the hospital or to the Commission but he would not. "I dare not go, for if my boss knew I had radiation sickness he might fire me as a bad risk."

The balance between reason and emotion is hard to maintain. Hiroshima maintains it perhaps better than the rest of the country. What Dr. Darling says of the newspapers is true. On the subject of radiation they are irresponsible. An article in the *Mainichi* is headed:

5 Years After Lucky Dragon Incident:

EX-CREW OF ILL-FATED SHIP
LEADING MISERABLE LIVES

The 22 former crew members of the tuna fishing boat No. 5 *Fukuryu Maru* (Lucky Dragon) are in miserable living conditions five years after they were affected by radioactivity as a result of a U.S. hydrogen bomb test in the southern Pacific. . . .

Careful reading of the story reveals that three are still fishermen, one lost his compensation money in an unsuccessful business venture and has since disappeared, sixteen have moved elsewhere and were not interviewed, one is unemployed. The only other striking point is that the other inhabitants of the town are jealous of the crew's compensation money.

Such is the attitude of the newspapers. The people of Hiroshima may feel differently. They do not use their misfortunes for propaganda.

Hiroshima is a bleak town. Its broad streets alone speak of the singular place it occupies in history. Its inhabitants, excepting those who still suffer and those who still work for the sufferers, prefer to forget.

In Peace Square one may meet with an old man who, for a few yen, will bare his back and show you his scars; but near where he stands the authorities paste up a warning that he is a rogue. As often as he tears it down, they replace it once more.

•   •   •

We drove down the coast southward from Hiroshima until we came to a small village opposite the island of Myajima. We left the car at the quayside because we were told it would cost $15 to transport it across to the island, and there was not above four miles of road over there in any case. The passenger ferryboat was surprisingly full considering this was not the tourist season. A man came around selling bottles of fizzy lemonade and was so put out when I didn't want one that he eventually persuaded me to buy some. It came in an intriguing bottle specially designed for drinking out of. There was a round glass ball in the neck, which once you had tilted the bottle prevented any of the liquid coming out. It was designed in this way so that you could adjust the flow into your mouth by pressing on the round ball with your tongue and allowing the lemonade to seep around it.

When we were halfway across the narrow straits between the island and the main shore we saw coming back another much more elaborate kind of ferryboat, with a beautiful carved prow in the shape of a dragon's head and a fancy cabin all done in fretwork and painted in garish colors. It looked more like a Chinese festival boat, and we were rather disappointed not to have waited a short while and taken it rather than the pedestrian baby steamer that we were on. This notion was slightly dispelled when, as the other boat drew level with ours, we heard blaring from the loudspeaker the words of an American song—"Sixteen, seventeen, hygiene baby."

The village on the island was almost deserted, for ours was nearly the last boat which would go back to the mainland that evening. The small street which led from the harbor through the main part of the village was geared entirely for tourists. The only houses on both sides were either hotels or souvenir shops selling toys, postcards, wooden spoons made out of cherry wood, carved deer, and painted towels—in fact, just what you would expect in any resort. The hotel keepers came rushing up to us as soon as they saw us, glad at the possibility of some custom at such an unlikely time of year. The island is famous for its cherry blossom and maples, so that the idea of anybody coming in the height of summer was obviously absurd. Nevertheless, they still asked for six dollars per night per person. We had very little money left, and determined, rather shamelessly, to trade on Japanese courtesy. We went into a likely looking hotel and chatted to the proprietor about this and that for ten minutes before even raising the question of rooms. And then we said that we would like to stay in his hotel for two dollars a night each. By this time some form of relationship had been established, and therefore he felt bound to agree, although I afterwards calculated that it could barely have been an economic rate for him, the more so as having come to the arrangement he gave us the same service and food as he would have given us for six dollars a head.

We had our bath, followed by a pleasant dinner—mostly fresh fish—and then, in our kimonos provided by the hotel, we went for a walk to have a look at the famous shrine. It was still light as we set off in the muted glow of evening. The village came to an abrupt end, and we were in an avenue of beautiful cedar trees, running along beside the water. To our left a steep bank climbed up to a high hill on which one could just see, between the trees, the shape of a pagoda. Spaced out along the shore were lichen-covered stone lanterns, and every so often we came across a small wooded temple building. The atmosphere was that of a park.

We walked slowly along the avenue for about a quarter of an hour until, on turning a corner, we found an inlet in the coast, and seemingly floating on the water of the bay the most perfect red shrine. It was built on stilts and when the tide is high they are quite concealed with the sea lapping almost over the boards of the shrine floor. A long wooden pier leads out into the sea and, just beyond the end of it, there stands in the water a high massive arch of wood known as a *torii.* The shrine, lying at the foot of the steep wooded valley, is one of the most romantic settings in all Japan.

The next morning we left for Shikoku. Finding a boat to take the car was difficult as there was no ferry from Hiroshima. At length we met a man who said he had a grain ship and he would be glad to take the motor as he was going to Shikoku without any cargo. We expected this to mean that he had a substantial sort of vessel, but after we had followed him down the quay for a way he pointed to a boat which was rather less than twice as long as the car. He said he could easily manage it and, as we had no alternative, we had to take his word for it. Straight away he called up some friends to help him load the car on to the little boat. There was no crane, and the operation was achieved with much shouting and yelling and little more in the way of mechanical help than three giant-sized knitting needles. The owner of the vessel would not hear of our going with him, because he said the journey would take him overnight, whereas we could catch a passenger boat in the morning which would reach Shikoku in about four hours. So we agreed to that and spent one more night in Hiroshima.

The journey in the ferryboat was extremely pleasant, leading as it did through the heart of the Inland Sea. We saw again the tiny islands, some with perfect, deserted beaches of pure white sand and even the smallest ones inhabited by a handful of people wherever there was a flat piece of land on which a living could be scratched. We arrived at Takahama at about four in the afternoon and were agreeably surprised to find that the car was waiting for us.

Martha was to catch a boat to take her back to Kyoto

while, with a friend, I went off to the seminar. We had a little
time to spare so we wandered around Matsuyama, the capital of Shikoku. Although much of the town was bombed and
has been rebuilt, in some districts with concrete buildings,
it is in some ways still primitive or, anyhow, unaffected by
Western civilization. In the back streets we discovered one
little shop which could never now exist in Tokyo or Kyoto.
At first sight it looked like a cross between a druggist's and a
taxidermist's, but on investigation it turned out to be a
virility shop. There, intermingled with perfectly ordinary
drugs, were phials of snake's blood, mysterious monkey ex-
tracts and herbal mixtures all openly advertised as increasing sexual potency. There were also small weird machines
intended for various sexual purposes. The majority of them
were designed for women. There were pills for speeding you
up and slowing you down. There was no attempt at conceal-
ment. The whole business was conducted in a perfectly
normal, open fashion and as naturally accepted as the fish
shop next door.

We took Martha back to the port to see her off on the
boat. The ship itself looked quite big, a little larger than a
channel steamer. At the ticket office, when I tried to buy a
first-class ticket for her, the man protested that it was a
ridiculous waste of money and that she would have a perfectly excellent cabin, probably to herself, so I bought a
second-class ticket. In the event this proved to be so. The
crowd on the pier was far greater than anything one would
see at Southampton when the *Queen Mary* leaves. There
were about two hundred passengers, and it seemed that not
less than three people had come to see off each of them. We

struggled on the boat through this jostling crowd, and having installed Martha got off again and waited for the ship to leave. All the passengers crowded the side of the ship and, shouting and yelling, threw down streamers of paper to their friends below. Each of us clutched on to a brightly colored ribbon, everyone crying final farewells as the ship steamed out and the passengers unrolled their coils of paper until, when the ship was about thirty yards out from the shore, the whole crowd seemed to be tugging her back, unwilling to be parted from their friends. I found out that although the ship leaves every night, every night there is the same touching farewell.

· · ·

We drove out of Kyoto straight up the hills behind our house, and were in the depths of the country within ten minutes. The road climbed half the way up to Mount Hiei, which dominates Kyoto from the northeast. There is a fork in the hills and we took the road which plunged down again to Lake Biwa—called so because its shape resembles that of an old musical instrument of that name. There is a superstition that the lake was formed at the same time as Mount Fuji in the gigantic earthquake. There is also off the coast near Kobe an island called Awaji, which is roughly the same shape as Lake Biwa and this island is supposed to have risen up at the same time as the lakeland sank.

We followed the shore in the direction of the Japan Sea. At this point the country is very narrow and it is possible to drive from one side of it to the other quite easily in one day. Starting as we did about halfway across, we reached the coast at Tsuruga, a dismal little town, at about four o'clock in the afternoon. I noticed that a great many of the shops had Russian signs over the doorways. Apparently there is a regular service from here to the U.S.S.R. There was nothing between us and Siberia. We had been told that the coast just north of this was extremely beautiful, though we were advised that it was probably better merely to look at it from the train, because there would be nowhere suitable to stay and the people were reportedly unattractive and primitive. Certainly as we left Tsuruga we realized that we were in a part of the country which was virtually untouched by any outside influence.

The dirt road, which in places was little more than a track, swooped up and down the rocky edge of the land. There were no gas pumps, no villas—nothing whatsoever excepting an occasional small fishing village amounting only to a cluster of houses and a fire tower, from which an eye could be kept on the whole community and the first trace of smoke reported by the loud clanging of a bell. There were narrow valleys with as many paddy fields clawed out of the steep land as possible. It was harvesttime and from the crest of each hill looking down on the next valley, one saw raised haphazardly over the fields twenty-foot-high racks on which were hung the sheaves of rice, carefully arranged so that each sheaf would dry in the wind.

After driving along for about an hour I became slightly perturbed at not finding any village big enough to have an inn. The word tourist cannot possibly have been known there. But the sea was beautiful, dotted about with rocks which would look improbable in a woodblock print so contrived were their shapes and, to complete their unreality, on some there grew one lone pine, leaning at an impossible angle and looking as if it had been pruned by a miniature-tree grower. Just when we were about to despair and were wondering whether to turn back or to camp out with no equipment, we came upon a most perfect bay with, at the far end, a bottle-shaped promontory. At the neck there was a village slightly larger than the ones we had seen before and beyond, where the land swelled out to form the body of the bottle, there rose a hill—round, with a temple on the top. The place was so beautiful that we decided we would stay there, whether there was an inn or not.

We drove on to the promontory until we came to the village and the street became so narrow that it was impossible to get the car any farther. We walked, followed by a crowd of awed school children, until we came out into the small harbor. Along the stony beach high-prowed fishing vessels were pulled up out of the water, fishing nets were hanging up to dry and, representing the other half of the villagers' livelihood, there were rice racks almost down to the water's edge. To one side of this port was a building slightly larger than the others, surrounded by a cluster of persimmon trees. It was an inn.

The chattering of the school children had already attracted the attention of everyone to our presence and when I went up to the inn door the old woman who appeared to run it knelt on the floor, touching the boards with her forehead.

"Am I right in thinking this is an inn?" I asked, for there

was no sign outside. The only way in which one could tell was from the long row of slippers on the threshold step.

The old woman spoke into the boards. "It is only a poor sort of inn," she said. "It is not suitable for you."

"But have you by any chance some rooms for us?"

"We have rooms, but we could not let them to you."

"I hope that we may persuade you to change your mind. This is such a beautiful place and we would love to stay here."

"No," she said.

It was almost the first time I had heard anybody use the actual word for "no," it being impolite to disagree.

"It is a hideous place. Just a wretched place tucked away in the country where no one could wish to stay."

"But we think it is a lovely place. We would so much like to stay in your inn, which looks so pleasant."

"No, it is not pleasant at all. It is a horrible house, old and shameful, and you could not possibly enjoy it."

In spite of all this I asked if we could see the rooms, and at last the old woman, who had throughout the conversation remained prostrate on the ground and had never once looked up, even when she spoke, got reluctantly to her feet. She led us off to two very simple but perfectly ordinary rooms, one with a long window overlooking the sea.

"But they are very nice rooms," I said.

"No, they are dreadful rooms, small, uncomfortable, dark and the *tatami* is worn. You could not possibly stay here."

I assured her that we could and that we fully intended to do so. How much, I asked, would they be?

"Six dollars," she said.

"Each?" I asked, a little surprised.

"Oh no," she said, quite scandalized. "For all four of you. And, of course, it includes dinner and breakfast. But I do not think you should stay here. We have never had foreigners to stay before and you will think us quite barbaric."

In the end we all agreed that we would stay, and the old woman bustled off to make certain that the bath was at least 120 degrees in honor of guests who came from the city and from a foreign land.

We spent an extremely comfortable night and the food was perfectly adequate except that the old woman decided that we must need fried eggs in the morning, for this was what she had heard all foreigners ate, so she prepared them with great care at about half past six in the morning and then kept them until eight o'clock, when we had ordered breakfast. I have never met such excessive politeness, and yet this is what Japan must have been like everywhere a hundred years ago. For it was not just the old woman who followed the ancient customs. In the morning, while the others climbed up to look at the temple, I sat on an upturned boat on the shore. Quite a young girl came by, carrying a small baby on her back. I said "good morning" to her and we talked for a short while. I asked her how old the baby was.

"Two," she said. As it was plainly not more than about six months old I was slightly confused until I remembered that by the old method of reckoning a child is one on the day it is born, and becomes two on the next New Year's Day. So a baby born on Christmas Day is two a week later.

"He is a very pretty baby," I said.

"No, no, he is repulsive," she answered. "I do not know

how my husband could be the father of such an ugly baby."

"Well, if you think he's so ugly," I said, "would you like to give him to me, because I think he's delightful."

"Ah, no," she said. "He's much too ugly to give away." Then she laughed at me.

•   •   •

As we were driving, we were drawn to go a little off the road by the sight of a mass of little girls in costume, evidently all dressed up for a festival in a small fishing village. We found that it was not due to start until the afternoon, but at the quayside we noticed considerable excitement at the return of a fishing vessel. We went down to see what was happening. They had had quite a good catch, which the crew quickly laid out on the quay. There was a swordfish, two hammer-headed sharks and a great number of smaller fish which I could not identify. They were all arranged in open boxes and divided for sale in lots. The few oddments which were left over, the five crewmen put into five baskets which they placed in a circle on the ground. They then all walked around and around the circle of baskets chanting a sad discordant song which got louder and louder as they went faster and faster. Abruptly they stopped, for no apparent reason and, each one grabbing the basket which was closest to him, set off home.

The captain of the ship did not go in for this game, but he stayed behind to conduct the auction. I have the impression that he must have seen a film of a tobacco sale in the States. He wore a pair of white breeches and stood swaggering in front of the fish boxes working himself up into a great fever of agitation and mock anger. Every so often he would swoop down on the boxes, striking them with a large metal hook. All this performance was rather wasted, for the only buyers were about half-a-dozen old women who had obviously known him since he was a little boy and were not in any way impressed by his rantings. On the other hand I feel they would have been most disappointed if he had not given of his best. The really puzzling aspect of the auction was the method of bidding, for while the captain made a wild excess of noise the buyers were totally silent. They each held in their hands a small piece of slate on which they scribbled their offer for each lot and showed it privately by the twist of a cupped hand to the auctioneer. It was very difficult to judge who bought each lot for all the auctioneer did was to glance at the slates and keep on yelling at an unintelligible rate. Then, at a given moment, all his spurious rage would disappear and he would move on, thump a few more boxes and start working himself up again.

. . .

We passed through Miyaza where Stubbs' [1] mother-in-law lives. I had hoped to call on her, for his description of the family's formality intrigued me, but it was impossible to find the house. The old woman keeps a strict hand on the household. When Stubbs last went to stay she told her daughter to tell him his bath was ready. Kei called up the stairs to him. The old woman was quite indignant at such casual behavior and made Kei go upstairs, get down on her knees, slide open

[1] An English friend with a Japanese wife.

the door of his bedroom and bowing, tell him formally that the bath was prepared.

The old woman herself had, naturally, had an arranged marriage. During her wedding day she had been too shy ever to look at her husband. In the morning she got up while it was still dark and went to make breakfast for the family. When the men came down to eat it, she had no idea which was her husband, and which her brother-in-law until a number of ribald jokes from the family made it plain to her.

*   *   *

By the time we reached Tottori we were back in the world to which we were accustomed. It is a hideous town, rebuilt about three years ago after a fire which devastated nearly two-thirds of its houses. It is a famous watering spot, with a large number of huge inns, each with its own hot-spring baths. They were nearly all full up and it took us some time to find one where we could stay. Once again we were among simpering, giggling girls who went off into hysterics every time I had to duck under a low doorway. The baths were communal ones which both men and women shared. They were scalding hot, and the little girls who shared it with us went off into peals of laughter watching us inch our way into the steaming water.

A few doors down from the bathroom there was a party of young men celebrating something or other with about six geisha girls to look after them. One of the boys was determined to practice his English with us.

"Harro, harro," he cried as he saw us going to the bath.

While we were drying he came along to talk to us. He was slightly drunk and inspected us with enormous care.

"What beautiful body you have," he said to my friend. And then, coming over to me, was about to say the same thing when some honesty broke through his drunkenness. Instead he reached up his hand on to my chest and said, "What lovely hair. You are very lucky to have such wonderful hair on your chest."

. . .

Arthur Koestler, who was in Japan for a few weeks, had asked us to make a journey with him to the western island of Kyushu. We left Kyoto at about ten o'clock on Tuesday morning.

It was luckily not the rush hour so we managed to get seats on the train without an excessive battle. Nevertheless, even though it was perfectly plain that there was plenty of room for everyone on the platform, there was a considerable scuffle at the door of the carriage, which we avoided by the simple expedient of waiting till the other passengers had got on and then peacefully going to the empty seats. The fact of having Arthur Koestler with us caused a certain amount of excitement. Various professors had come to see him off and, several times on the journey, when we stopped at university towns, someone would get on and pay his respects to Arthur during the short wait at the station.

We got to Kurashiki at about midday, and were met by three or four photographers and two journalists carrying a tape recorder. They asked Arthur if he would give them an interview, and he said that he was merely making a private visit to Japan and, on the whole, would rather not make any particular statement. But the young men were very persistent and begged him just to say a few words. He finally agreed to this, whereupon the boys switched on their apparatus and thrusting up the microphone to his mouth said:

"What are your impressions of Kurashiki?"

Very reasonably Arthur pointed out that, as all we had seen of Kurashiki was the platform on which we stood, he was hardly in a position to express any opinion whatever.

"Go away for a few minutes," he said, "and think up a few more intelligent questions and I will be happy to answer them."

We went to the station to check our bags, as we were going on that evening by a night train to the west. When we had done this, the journalists came back bubbling with a new confidence and declared that they were ready with their questions.

"Very well," said Arthur. "What are they?"

"First," said the boys, "what are your impressions of Kurashiki?"

They did not get any interview.

The town of Kurashiki is virtually dominated by a Mr. Ohara who owns a large rayon factory. His father must have been a man of some enterprise, for in the town there are three museums of considerable importance, all of them founded by him. The present Mr. Ohara had very kindly arranged for a car to be put at our disposal, and for Mr. Tonomura—the director of one of the museums—to guide us around. I had met him before on a previous visit to Kurashiki and he was quite overwhelming in his welcome to us. He took us first of all to the main inn of the town and gave us the most delicious luncheon. I noticed with some surprise that there were in the inn six replicas of Windsor chairs. I asked about these and was told that they had been made to the design of Bernard Leach, who is regarded in Japan as almost the savior of folk craft.

The corner of Kurashiki where the inn was placed was quite unlike any other Japanese town. Through this section there ran a canal, spanned by two or three attractive arched bridges. The houses on either side were not the usual drab brown wooden structures, but instead stuccoed houses with a raised green diamond pattern on them. They gave the quarter an unusual air of permanence, which one misses in the average town.

Mr. Tonomura had set aside the whole day for our entertainment and seemed quite undaunted by the prospect of having to look after four strangers for twelve hours without interruption. He took us next to the most surprising of the museums.

A few hundred yards up the road across the canal from the inn stands a mock-classical building made of stone. I had been to it before and knew that it contained a collection, made by the first Mr. Ohara, of modern French paintings. Arthur Koestler was a little hesitant about going there, holding the view that he had not come right around the world in order to see something which he could find perfectly well at home. But after two minutes in the place he agreed that it was more than worth while. It is a strange fact that in the early nineteen-twenties a Japanese industrialist should have built up a collection of French paintings which would be a considerable addition to any European gallery. It is true that there are a few indifferent paintings, by artists of whom I have never heard, but a collection which can provide two Picassos, a Braque, two Rouaults, a Monet and a Matisse, a Vlaminck and a Léger, a Van Gogh and a Cézanne, not to mention pictures by Pissarro, Vuillard, Bonnard, Segonzac, Toulouse-Lautrec, Gauguin—nearly all of a high standard— is a remarkable find twelve thousand miles from Paris.

Mr. Tonomura then took us to his own museum, which he has created entirely himself. It is a collection of folk art, and one of the very few of its sort in the country. It is true that Bernard Leach, who is a great friend of Tonomura's, did much just before the war to inspire an interest among the Japanese in their native crafts. Until that time the only thing that anyone had thought worth collecting was the traditional fine art of the country. It is an excellent thing that some interest has been aroused, for the fine arts, at any rate those most admired by the Japanese themselves, however great their excellence, are mainly derived from the Chinese, whereas the folk art reveals a certain original vigor which many Western people are facilely prepared to deny exists.

After about three hours of museums we all felt inclined for some simple time-consuming relaxation, for there were still seven hours before our train was due to go. Mr. Tonomura was dutifully anxious to show us around the rayon factory, but rather ungratefully we told him this would be very tedious and quite shamelessly persuaded him to drive us some fifteen miles to the Inland Sea, which Arthur Koestler would otherwise never have seen. After about three-quarters of an hour's drive, so bad were the roads, we reached the coast. It was teeming with rain, but this in the end proved to be rather satisfactory. Once again I noticed forcibly how much more stylized is the landscape of Japan than the familiar woodblock prints which represent it. The islands, sprinkled in the misty sea, look even more romantic and improbable than any print, and Mr. Tonomura with his love of the traditional, quite forgave us for the fact that we had dragged him out for a long drive against his will. The view which we saw, unspoiled and untouched, represented the exact world to which he had given up his life. It showed the old Japan, simple and romantic, which had given birth to the folk art he so loved. By the end of the afternoon he was positively grateful.

He took us back to Kurashiki and to his own house, which was a few doors down from the inn where we had had lunch. The house was virtually an extension of the museum, filled with bits of cloth woven in one prefecture, pots thrown in another, scrolls from Korea, roof tiles from Okinawa, rice pestles and kettles—in fact everything collected from anywhere that Japan had at any time governed.

Somehow it wasn't until we got into the house that we fully realized what a delightful collector's item Mr. Tonomura was himself. He was tall for a Japanese, with a great shock of white hair. His face had some of the quality of vellum and on his nose he wore a most intriguing pair of spectacles. The lenses were on a hinge, and when he wanted to look at something at a distance he would raise the lenses up so that they stuck out at right angles to his forehead, but when he wanted to read he would lower them. Somehow the clip mechanism didn't seem to work properly and the lenses flapped up and down with every movement of his head. He was dressed in layers of loosely woven kimonos which he made himself on his handloom and dyed with dark rich vegetable coloring. He had that less strenuous but more perfect courtesy of the older generation and that same, more direct, uninhibited intelligence that Mrs. Kazama, our landlady, had. Certainly there is the involved complication of the web of obligation which one feels that no Japanese can ever throw off, but there is a freedom of expression and attitude which one never finds among the younger people. He was touching in his enthusiasm at our interest.

From everywhere all over the house he dragged out all manner of objects to illustrate the points that he was making. In the middle of this his wife, a much younger woman and attractive, produced an elaborate dinner for us. I told her that I remembered the delicious plum wine which she had given me on my previous visit. She appeared very miserable that they had drunk it all up, but produced instead a rather sweet but extremely good wine which she made from grapes. There were piles and piles of sliced *sukiyaki* beef and what appeared to be the product of a whole acre of vegetable growing. The Tonomuras cannot have been rich, but for this dinner party they provided more meat than a whole Japanese family would ordinarily have eaten in a month.

Even after dinner was over there were still some hours before our train was due to leave, but Mr. Tonomura would not hear of our going out to wait in a café or a cinema as we proposed.

He announced that he would play us some records of

folksongs from all over Japan. He went to a cupboard and produced a portable gramophone which appeared to be about thirty years old. A great show was made of choosing which record we should listen to first, and then it was placed on the turntable and Mr. Tonomura began to wind up the machine. He whirled the handle with enormous energy for what seemed a very long time. Then, just as we expected, there came the most fearful click and whirring from the inside of the motor. Mr. Tonomura appeared not to notice, but took it for a signal to put on the record. He flicked the turntable and the record slowly and deliberately turned two revolutions and then stopped. We preserved reasonably straight faces, and Mr. Tonomura proceeded to wind it up again.

We all waited, and sure enough, after a while, there was a sinister scrunch from the spring and Mr. Tonomura beamingly applied the needle to the record once again with the same cacophonous result. This time our smiles grew a bit broader. Mr. Tonomura called the maid in and asked her what had happened, giving her a third demonstration of how the thing worked. The maid explained that it was broken, a ruling which Mr. Tonomura was not prepared to accept. He put the needle on the record again and proceeded to wind with ferocious energy. By this system the record would go gradually faster and faster until the spring gave its whirring noise and the turntable slowed down almost to nothing. The more often it happened the more ferociously Mr. Tonomura wound. There was this figure, dressed in folkweave clothes, with his wild spectacles flapping up and down, a figure straight from the prints of Hokusai, winding feverishly away at a twentieth-century machine, albeit thirty years old. It was a sight altogether too much for us and we collapsed, giving up all pretence of politeness, and the more we laughed the more Mr. Tonomura wound until eventually even he was so overcome with giggling that he finally had to give up the enterprise and we spent the rest of the evening until our train left, looking at lantern slides.

.   .   .

After a morning wandering about Fukuoka, recovering from an overnight journey, we took the train on to Nagasaki. We were in a second-class compartment, arranged much like a Pullman carriage on an English train. On the other side of the gangway was a young couple plainly on their honeymoon. They were both dressed in brand-new clothes and looked mildly out of place in their Western styles. They hardly spoke to one another. The young man had a small transistor radio which he played ceaselessly throughout the whole journey. Every so often the girl would try to distract him with some remark, but he merely nodded or grunted and looked away again and continued to listen to his radio. She tried every kind of diversion, even reading to him little bits out of the railway timetable and roaring with laughter at each item she found in it. He listened, without once smiling or answering, until finally she bothered no more and made little paper cranes out of silver paper. When she had made one, she put in on the window ledge and pointed it out to her husband, who treated it with the same contempt that he had the sallies from the railway timetable. Feverishly she made more and more cranes, until quite a row of them stood on the ledge. After about three hours we prepared to get out. He still showed no interest in the cranes she had made, but stood there waiting for her to help him on with his coat, and then allowed her to carry all the baggage off the train.

We hired a car to drive out from Nagasaki to Obama, which we had been told was a wonderful hot-spring resort farther along the coast. Driving through the countryside of this westernmost island it seemed almost to be a totally different country. Although it was still early spring, the valleys were already green with the early rice crop. There were oranges still on the trees and beautiful flowering shrubs in full bloom, giving Kyushu an almost tropical air. The coast, like so much of the shoreline of Japan, reminded me of an untouched Riviera, with twisted pine trees making grotesque patterns on the cliffs overhanging the sea. Nothing is developed, and the villages we drove through were much the same as they have always been.

Obama, when we reached it, was little more than a fishing village, with at one end a sprouting of new hotels. For some reason or other we had gone against our usual rule of hunting for an unlikely inn and had booked ourselves rooms in one recommended by the Tourist Bureau. It was in a pleasant enough place, looking over the sea toward the north where Nagasaki lay, a view which one of the older fishermen told me he had looked at in disbelief on the night of the dropping of the second atom bomb, certain that the end of the world had come.

The inn itself was still in the process of being enlarged and we were given a choice of a number of new rooms. They were decorated in a hideous fashion, combining all the worst features of Western design with an over-rusticated Japanese traditional style. The inn girls, who were of a fatuity that I had seldom seen surpassed, took one look at Arthur Koestler and said they had just the room for him. His sitting room was passable enough, with a green carpet laid over the *tatami* matting and a twisted varnished pillar made from a pine branch in the traditional recess. But the bedroom was something which I had never expected to see. There was no furniture except for an enormous double bed. The walls and ceiling were made of looking glass. There was no window. The only light was provided by four naked bulbs of different colors hung round a large revolving globe of mirrors. Rather indignantly, Arthur asked to be removed to another room.

The food, on the other hand, was rather good and the hot-spring baths quite delightful. There was one large bath indoors in which one could swim at least ten strokes, and another out of doors slightly marred by the fact that it was separated from the sea-front road only by a low wall and that at one end men were always at work drawing off the water and drying it out in order to extract some special salt or sulfur which was considered salubrious.

On the second day there we decided to take the bus up to Unzen, a mountain that has the reputation of being one of the most beautiful in Japan. Although it was off season, a bus left every twenty minutes and each one was packed. They were extremely comfortable, and we settled down to enjoy ourselves. We had hardly moved a few hundred yards when the bus conductress, who was dressed in a trim blue uniform and cap of the kind that one normally associates with airline hostesses, started to address us over the loudspeaker system. As the bus swayed around the hairpin bends of the steep, climbing road, she stood on the platform behind the driver with one hand clinging onto a rail and the other clutching a microphone. She had a curiously high-pitched, slightly whining voice, and she talked in a super-polite language which I had imagined was really only used to address princesses.

The views as we climbed higher and higher were quite spectacular, but the effect was spoiled by this voice scratching out dreary information mostly connected with some obscure detail of history or alternatively describing the amenities of a new bath house which we were just passing, but which presumably none of us would ever have the opportunity of using. Then, too, at selected points she would break into songs purporting to be the traditional airs of that vicinity. Even this taxed one's credence slightly because until very recent times no one could have lived there because most of these parts were only readily accessible as the result of modern engineering and road building. Moreover the words of the songs which she sang in her raucous whine were of a particular idiocy that could only have been devised by writers of this decade. They were on the lines of:

> *Beautiful, beautiful Obama,*
> *We have left thee far behind;*
> *Climbing as we are to the mountain*
> *Of glorious, glorious Unzen.*

At the village of Unzen, which looked like a development contractor's vision of St. Moritz, we had to get out and change buses. Once again we swooped up twisty mountain roads, the land beside us now barren and innocent of trees, to the accompaniment of more information and snatches of song. At last we reached the point where the bus could go no farther. There was about a hundred-yard walk to the foot of a cable-car railway, but as this was a famous spot, almost of pilgrimage, no diversion was spared. Waiting at the bus stop were a number of mangy horses which one could ride over the patch to the cable-car station, provided, I imagine, in case *ennui* should come upon one in those few moments of walking when there was no loudspeaker to tell one where one was or to drug one with information.

The cable car climbed the last three or four hundred feet to the summit of the mountain. In spite of the rain and mist the view was certainly remarkable. We were about 4,000 feet above Obama and we could see the sweep of land leading up to Nagasaki in one direction and down to Shimabara and Hozu, where the persecuted Christians of Kyushu made their last stand after the Shogun's edict outlawing them in the seventeenth century.

At the summit there was a platform with four positions from which one could see the views best. Each point was numbered, and everyone from the cable car went religiously first to Point One and then Point Two and so on, with the result that they had to jump up and down to see over one another. Arthur very intelligently suggested that if we went the other way around we would manage the whole thing more comfortably save for a mild scrimmage between Points Three and Two. This we did, and the maneuver met with

furious mutterings and stares of indignation at such devia-
tionist activities.

We then journeyed back to Obama by the same route with
the exception of one small diversion and were the whole way
treated to either a further elaboration or exactly the same
stories as those we had heard on the way up. I was too
exhausted by the voice to listen hard enough to discover
which.

CHAPTER NINE

FESTIVALS

F ESTIVALS play a direct part in the life of the Japanese. It is very rare to go on a journey of more than two or three days' driving without coming upon a procession of Shinto priests in red and yellow costumes following a portable shrine, or of children in old-fashioned kimonos or of Buddhist monks on some short pilgrimage. This passion for religious fancy dress is a manifestation of the strong hold which tradition has over the people. It is part and parcel of the same conditioning which makes the Japanese pepper their conversation with foreigners with phrases starting "we have a saying" or "it is said from olden times." It is the same influence which makes them all remember their fairy tales and prompts them to quote constantly illustrations from their history.

Every schoolboy does genuinely know the most useless information dragged from the annals of Japanese history. All conversation with foreigners turns at one stage or another to the traditions and customs of the country. It is as if everyone in England, on meeting someone from abroad, were to be forever drawing on anecdotes from Shakespeare, Hall's *Chronicles* and Beowulf to illustrate each point in his conver-

sation. Among the young there is an obsession with everything modern and Western. But in everyone there lingers an
uneasy respect for the past. At the same time there is a
prettiness in their observance of rites which have long since
lost their meaning.

In Kyoto there are two main festivals—the Gion *matsuri*
and the Jidai *matsuri*—which are long processions involving
hundreds of people in fancy dress—both connected with
Shinto shrines. But these two are so elaborate as to be dull
and really only of interest to tourists, although nearly everyone automatically turns out to see them.

But more attractive are the little festivals at the lesser-
known shrines, in particular those just outside Kyoto. One
of the most vivid is the Fire Festival at Kurama, a small village in the hills to the north of the city. The stories of its origin are rather vague. One attributes its importance, if not its
actual beginnings, to the fact that the nephew of one of the
Shoguns was imprisoned in this village and managed to
escape during the festival. But it is plain to see that the customs now observed there in October of every year are direct
relics of fertility rites and sacrifices.

The whole village street is lit with bonfires spaced out at
intervals of about fifty yards and the evening starts with the
young men of the village careering around the square with
enormous flaming torches, so heavy that it takes two men
to carry them. The torch bearers wear little but a loincloth
with a swinging fringe, a thin open-fronted jacket and a
headband. The crowd is thick, and the men rush about in
its midst swaying unsteadily with a curious thrusting side-
step, whirling their heavy brands so that the sparks scatter

everywhere, and, as they turn, the faces of the crowd near the fire are suddenly lit up in an ecstatic moment of fear before they dash backward, trampling one another in their panic. It is not a night for those less nimble to wander in the streets.

All the houses are open, their fronts removed to expose the living rooms with all the family treasures on view—here a carpet from China or a Korean tea bowl and there a suit of *samurai* armor or a set of special lacquer trays. Hospitality is unending, and the only closed houses are those in which there has been a death in the past year.

As in all Japanese festivals and other entertainments the whole thing takes a prodigious length of time. The preliminaries go on for at least two hours, until, at midnight, two groups of priests from the temple high up on the hill above the village meet together in the square and from the groups of youths choose two boys of about sixteen. At this moment, the young men with their brands range themselves on the lowest of the long flight of hundreds of steps, resting the bottom end of their torches between their feet and leaning the flaming end at an angle in front of them, so that they have to pull with all their strength to keep the brands from falling forward and in their rows they make a moving pagan sight of near-naked sweating youthful bodies straining in the firelight. Their ranks part, and the two selected boys are rushed up the steps into the darkness, up toward the temple.

I went to this festival with a priest from a Zen monastery, and tried to get some enlightenment from him as to what sort of religious principles were involved.

"It *is* a Buddhist temple up there?" I asked him.

"Oh, yes, certainly—Shingon sect."

"Well, this does not seem very much like a Buddhist ritual
to me."

"Ah, no?"

"No. And what are we waiting for now?"

"Soon they will bring down the shrine containing the god."

He said these last words in English, because, I think, he
would have been rather at a loss to explain which god or
spirit was likely to come down from the Buddhist temple had
he stuck to Japanese.

"Why do they bring the god down?"

"Ah, once a year he likes an outing," he said facetiously.

More explanation than this I was unable to get. After a
long wait in the light of the bonfires and torches we could at
last see coming down the steep slopes of the steps a palanquin with long shafts carried by more youths dressed in the
same way as the torch bearers. As it came closer I could see
that between the front shafts was also carried, face down-
ward, a completely naked boy. Every so often his bearers
would turn him over and shove him upward so that the
crowd could see him. The palanquin was followed by a long
stream of people holding fast to a rope which was used to
steady the palanquin as it was brought down the steps.
Among those who held the rope were some girls. This was
the only part that women were allowed to play in the festival. Those who were actually carrying the palanquin moved
with that same sideways-thrusting gesture that the torch
bearers had used. It was somehow a provocative step,
charged with sexuality, and must also have given the god
an extremely uncomfortable ride, the more so because every

few yards the young men would shudder the palanquin, making its dangling metal decorations dindle and glitter in the firelight.

After the first palanquin came a second, also preceded by a naked sacrificial boy.

"They do not kill them any more," the priest said to me by way of explanation, and added rather whimsically that they were quite likely to die of pneumonia in any case.

The palanquins were carried to an open-sided building around which everyone danced and sang, getting drunker and drunker until at about two or three in the morning they struggled again up the long steep steps to return the gods to their temple at the end of their annual outing.

The charm of this festival lay in its naturalness. The boys taking part seemed, even if they did not understand its significance, to enjoy it and to be genuinely involved in the curious rites. In this they were quite unlike the young men who paraded in the long Kyoto processions, puffing at cigarettes and chattering to one another, oblivious of their part in the ceremony, interested only in the sixty cents they earned for their appearance.

This small country festival inspired me with a desire to go and see a larger performance of the same kind, also held in a temple of the Shingon sect, in a less-frequented part. This one took place at the coldest time of the year—in February—and, rather regretting leaving our warm house, I set off for Saidaiji, a small town about one hundred miles west of Kyoto. I drove down with two Japanese friends—one the husband of our cook and the other an official of the City Hall. It was a hideous journey, for the roads in the winter can

become almost impassable. As we were climbing a pass in
the mountains not far from Ako, where we had spent the
night on the beach in the summer, the road became a deep
slough of mud and, at a moment where we had not seen a
house for five miles, a hideous grinding crunch came from
underneath the car and we came to a painful stop, with our
wheels half obscured by thick red mud. There were still
about forty miles to go and I was in despair at the thought
of missing this festival. But it is at just such moments as these
that the Japanese become infinitely helpful. After considerable oohings and aahings and gruntings and groanings over
the miseries of such a predicament, they will set to without
any thought for their convenience or comfort and make the
best of it.

After various sorties in various directions, we had to admit
that the car wouldn't recover that day, and rather guiltily
Mr. Yamaguchi and I abandoned the cook's husband, who
prepared to take the car to pieces and find out what new
parts were necessary. Yamaguchi hailed a passing truck and
explained the position to the driver who agreed to drive us
as far as possible toward Saidaiji, and my last sight of Naka-
gawa was of him lying full length in the mud removing the
differential.

The day seemed to be full of kindness, for the truck driver,
seeing that we were worried about the time, drove a good
twenty miles out of his way over atrociously narrow roads,
which could hardly contain his huge vehicle, into the thick
of the crowded festival town in order to make sure we should
miss nothing. We had, in rather an improvident fashion,
planned to sleep in the car, so Mr. Yamaguchi and I had to

try and find accommodation in the packed hotels. When we told one of them that we had said to the beleaguered Naka-gawa that he would find us at this particular inn they felt so overwhelmed by our problems that they said we could sleep in the dancing room at the hotel. It was a peculiar room with a bar in one corner, and only a revolving colored globe for a light. I noticed on the walls a sign in Japanese saying: INSTRUCTIONS HOW TO USE THE DANSU HŌRU. There seems to be no word in Japanese for dance hall. However, we did not care and were delighted to find anywhere to sleep. After a quick dinner we went into the town.

Saidaiji is a small place, hardly warranting the title of city which has been given it. The town is placed on the banks of a wide river, not far from where it flows out into the sea. At the edge of the river is a small temple with a pagoda dedicated to Kannon, the Goddess of Mercy. The origin of the temple is obscure, there being two or three theories about its foundation. The first one is concerned with a religious old woman called Minatari-hime. She lived in the Nara dy-nasty, somewhere about the year 750. She had a desire to carve an image of Senju Kannon (the thousand-headed God-dess of Mercy) and to dedicate a temple to it.

Another theory was that the image of Kannon was origi-nally in a great temple some distance away but got washed away in a flood and brought here by the waters, and that the villagers then built a temple for it. There were versions con-cerned more directly with the actual building of the temple. It seems that about twenty years after Minatari-hime, a priest called Anryu had a divine revelation instructing him to re-build the humble thatched temple built by the old woman.

While he was journeying about by sea he passed through a strait where the tide suddenly went out and, on the sandy floor of the sea, appeared the palace of the Dragon King. The king came out of the palace and gave him a rhinoceros horn, telling him to bury it and build a temple on it. So Anryu went on to Kanaoka-no-so and buried his horn and called the temple which he built on it Saidaiji, which can signify rhinoceros horn. In fact the characters now used to write Saidaiji are not those which mean rhinoceros, but other ones, pronounced in the same way, meaning west great temple. Among the old records of the temple is one dated 1433, which says that the name was changed according to an Imperial Epistle.

There are more theories, too, about the change of a name but it seems most likely that at one time or another some manifestos had to be issued in a hurry and the characters of rhinoceros were so complicated that they adopted the simpler ones with a different meaning. That so many theories exist is proof of the love of virtually meaningless stories; however, I think that the rhinoceros horn is of some significance.

We found the street jammed with people, all pressing toward the temple. The whole compound was so thickly massed that it was hard to push one's way to the main building. Eventually, after about twenty minutes, Mr. Yamaguchi and I arrived at the back of the building, where a row of monks were sitting at a table selling tickets to those who wanted to pass through the main hall where the festival took place. By this time a number of people who were actually to take part in the rites were gathering. They were nearly all boys between the ages of sixteen and twenty, though among them there were a few older men. But no women. No one wore more than a small loincloth. They clustered together in little groups, linking arms and running around and around to keep warm in the February night air, shouting with the same rhythmic thudding sound that I had heard at Kurama, but here the word repeated over and over again was different. At Kurama it had been *Sai-rei, Sai-ryo.* Here it was *eyo, eyo, eyo, eyo.* They ran around for some time in the crowd, which parted whenever a group of them came toward it. At length they started to gravitate toward a small pool by the riverside. Into this the boys ran in an atavistic act of purification, for none of them seemed to take seriously whatever religious significance there may have been in their acts.

At one end of the pool was a small statue of Kannon carved in a decidedly phallic shape. Some of the boys seemed to realize this and rushed through the water toward it and wrapped their legs around the base of the statue crying out "look what I've got!" Once out of the water they rushed around in circles again, always crying *"eyo, eyo."* The groups of boys got larger and larger and gradually they all converged upon the temple itself.

This temple was built in two halves under a large sweeping roof. One half was devoted mostly to an altar, whereas the other was more like a huge veranda, open on three sides, with thick round pillars supporting the roof. The whole of this veranda can not have been more than about eight feet long by thirty feet broad. By now there were about a thousand near-naked boys and they all pressed and thronged to climb the steps on to the platform. The crowd in the veranda was unimaginable. One could no longer approach it from the front, so I went back to the place where the monks were selling tickets which allowed you to go into the back of the temple, past the altar, then up a narrow ladder to a balcony which ran around above the veranda to another exit at one side of the temple. One was supposed only just to walk through and to keep moving, but I persuaded the temple officials to allow me to stand at the foot of the stairway which led to the balcony, beside a wide, open archway looking on to the veranda. The boys were now so thickly packed that to prevent them being pressed through the arch they put up a thick wooden grille, and through this I was able to watch the proceedings.

With me, at an upright desk, stood two temple officials. On the desk were a number of long octagonal boxes with a hole at one end. The officials offered these boxes to the line of people waiting to climb up to the veranda. Many took a box, paid the official about five cents and shook the box until an ivory spilikin appeared through the hole. Each spilikin was numbered and the official would give the person a folded piece of paper with a corresponding number.

These pieces of paper were fortunes with the same style of information you find in a party snapper. But it was not always so cheerful. There were as many sighs from the purchasers as smiles, and it is customary for people for whom ill luck is foretold to hang the bad news on the twig of a tree in the hope that the wind will blow away the threatened misfortune.

The whole mass of boys was now shouting louder and louder "*eyo, eyo*" and, as more of them pressed in from outside, they started to climb up the grille to a ledge which ran around just below the balcony and even to scramble on to the huge beams which ran across below the roof. At length the whole of my grille was obscured by twisted, clinging, naked bodies, and in order to see anything I had to climb up the inside and try and look over their heads. The shouting of the boys settled into a drumming rhythmic beat which lost all relation to the human voice. It became almost like the mating call of some giant passionate monster. The tense crescendo of sexual fervor built up and up until one could not believe that it could last longer without some hideous climax. The boys became wilder in their beat-stressed sway-ing and more and more of them climbed up onto the ledges and into the roof and, reaching the beams, they displaced those that were there before them so that they jumped down from heights of ten to fifteen feet into the seething mass of bodies beneath them with no regard at all for those on whom they landed. From each section of the crowd would come a ghastly low cry as a body thumped down into their midst and, slowly sinking between them, became just another part of the sea of flesh.

Meanwhile, not thirty feet from this mad orgiastic scene, was an atmosphere of unbelievable calm. In the chapel just beside where I stood, ten monks and the abbot were conduct-ing a quiet Buddhist service. The abbot sat on one side of a huge low square table. He wore a vivid red robe. Opposite him was the altar, and five monks sat on the other two sides, dressed in white. Behind the abbot were a number of boys. The table was laden with offerings from the people of the town and the surrounding countryside. The monks appeared to be quite unaware of the wild shouting of the boys on the veranda. For about three hours they sat cross-legged on the floor chanting the *sutras*, reciting prayers, and occasionally beating on the table with short sticks which they picked up from the floor beside them for this purpose. The acolyte monks behind the abbot would occasionally break into some religious song, while the abbot himself told his beads like a rosary, occasionally rubbing them between his hands in a symbolic erasing of the one hundred and eight sins of mankind.

I wandered to and fro between the grille, behind which was the pressed contorted mass of limbs, and this peaceful scene of quiet devotion. From time to time, one of the boys on the veranda would reach through and ask me for a cigarette. I would light him one and pass it to him and watch with fascination as he struggled to get his hand to his mouth in order to puff at it. I did this once or twice but gave up when I saw one boy stub the cigarette out on another one's behind.

"Danger of fire," he yelled, when I tried to remonstrate with him, having sorted out which face belonged to the hand. It must be said in his defense that, in the frenzy and turmoil, his victim did not appear to wince, let alone complain.

After this I went back and talked to a monk of a different sect who was watching the service as a spectator like myself.

"Do you understand what this is all about?"

"Oh, yes."

"What is the significance of the service?"

"Ah, they are chanting the *sutras*," he said.

"They must be doing more than that, the chanting of the

sutras is a regular practice. There must be some connection between the service and the throng of boys."

"Oh, no, they just chant the *sutras*."

"What does that do?"

"There is much evil out in the hall. The abbot is getting rid of it."

"Is that all that he is doing?"

"Yes, Buddhism is a peaceful religion. All we try and do is cast out evil."

It was now about twelve-thirty, and it seemed that the climax of the festival usually came at about one o'clock, though this apparently depended entirely on the whim of the abbot. By this time the stream of people who had paid to be allowed to walk past where I was standing and climb up on to the balcony and out again and beyond had stopped. I had a typical Japanese argument with the officials at the foot of the steep ladder which led to the gallery because I asked them if I could just go up, look over, and come down again, to which their answer was that if I once went up the ladder I must go out beyond like everyone else. I pointed out that I had already been given special permission to stand where I was and that anyhow to go up and come back again was not a very serious affair, and furthermore that since they had stopped letting anyone through there would be nobody to complain. At length some Boy Scouts, who were rather unexpectedly employed by the temple as ushers for the evening, persuaded the officials that it was all right.

I climbed the ladder and stood on the balcony about twenty feet above the fantastic sea of boys below. Sea in this case is not a cliché. There below me was an undulating al-

most unformed mass bearing some resemblance to a Hierony-
mus Bosch, but more exaggerated than any painting by him
of hell. The bodies were so merged into one another, so
tightly crushed, that it was only the black heads of the boys
which gave the solid block of flesh any form. Without the
heads it would at first sight have seemed as though one were
looking down on a waving sea anemone. The whole swayed
from side to side, a convulsed wave, first one way and then
the other, the black heads like black flotsam, and from the
surface as one looked longer one noticed the boys' hands
reaching up like shocked fronds. They have to keep their
hands above their heads, or otherwise the pressure of the
crowd would squeeze them down and they would be
trampled upon, unable ever to escape.

From up here I could see better the boys who had climbed
up into the rafters for a moment's rest. There they would
sit, clinging to a beam till other boys climbed up and ousted
them. Then they would jump unconcernedly into the mass
once more.

One became aware of another strange aspect. Beside me
on the balcony were Buddhist novices with buckets of water.
Every so often they would fling a bucketful over the boys
below. As the water hit the bodies there was a loud hiss,
and steam rose in a dense cloud. The hiss, I suppose, was the
intake of breath from the impact of the sudden cold, but the
steam was real enough and the impression given was that of
water striking red-hot metal. So much so that a camera lens
was quickly clouded over.

When I had been up there about three minutes the officials
began to get agitated and I had to go down again to my

watching post behind the grille. The boys seemed to sense that the climax was near, so I went back into the shrine, rather dazed by what I had seen, to find the monks still continuing with their quiet service.

At last, there came a variation in their service from the normal ritual. They wrapped up pieces of paper in a sheaf of leaves and stuffed them into the sleeves of their kimonos. They they stood up and in slow procession, headed by the abbot, they climbed the ladder on to the balcony where I had stood. As soon as the boys below realized they were there the beating yells became louder and louder until it seemed that the noise of the boys' voices, hoarse and vibrant, would bring down the roof of the building. The monks threw down their scraps of leaf-wrapped scriptures and the crowd pressed in from outside the building, cramming the boys' bodies even more tightly. For a moment the lights were put out. During the seconds of darkness the abbot drew from his robes a short stick and flung it down among the crowd. The yelling suddenly became shrill and fevered and one wondered how the boys had strength to yell any more.

After the few instants of shrieking darkness the lights came on again and the throng of boys was now alive with a throbbing pulsating struggle. They yelled and pushed and struck out, each one striving to move in the direction where he felt the stick had fallen.

The abbot came slowly down the ladder and went back again to his place at the table. This time the monks did not sit with him, but hurried away. He sat alone and dignified, while the screaming of the boys continued unceasing, silently counting his beads and rubbing them between the open palms of his hands. Then he rose, smiled rather amiably at me and went out at the back of the building, quite unhurried.

I returned to the grille and found that already the crowd of boys had begun to thin. Evidently one of them had found the stick. Now the mass of them were milling fiercely in the compound at the front of the temple, shouting to one another, "Over there, over there!" and surging wherever they thought the holder of the stick might have gone. By the time I got out into the compound the abbot had taken up his place in a building beside the pagoda, where he waited until the victor should bring him the piece of wood.

Quite suddenly it was all over. A boy reached him with the stick and there was nothing more to be done. The crowd subsided abruptly into a curious apathy. It was almost as if they had experienced a massive communal orgasm. I have never seen a crowd disperse so quickly. There was no talking it over. They just went swiftly and quietly away. The boys, too, dressed hurriedly and vanished as rapidly as the spectators. There was no aftermath, no frivolity. It was just over.

The comparison with an orgasm is not so farfetched. The whole evening had had a blatantly sexual atmosphere about it. It was not merely libidinous, as the evening at Kurama had been, but rather an overwrought, tense experience.

The word *eyo* is of uncertain origin. It could perhaps mean quite simply "meet the sun," and the sun, of course, has a male significance. Or, depending on the reading of the character, it has been suggested that there is a definite connection with the word for phallus. I was told also that at one time the stick thrown down by the abbot used to be a carved representation of a phallus. The history behind all this is

almost impossible to get at without a great deal of research
and considerably more knowledge than I have of the subject,
but I cannot help feeling, and many Japanese that I talked
to agreed with me, that there must be some connection between this phallicism and the rhinoceros horn with all its
connotations of sex.

If one asks the origin of the festival and the casting in of
the stick one is told that at one time a piece of paper used to
be thrown down but that this was apt to get torn in the
crush. This seems to be a typical piece of Japanese white-
washing for the benefit of Westerners. But even they agree
that the piece of paper was meant to bring to the winner of
the struggle prosperity and fertility for his farm. This is still
supposed to be the case, although the boys are now more inclined to be interested in the three hundred dollars which
is given by the owners of a factory in Saidaiji, as a prize.

Certainly the festival must have its origins in a fertility
rite. The Shingon sect to which the temple belongs is the
sect of Buddhism which grafted most freely into its teach-
ings and practices the original religions of Japan. Since these
had chiefly an agricultural basis it seems likely that the
festival at Saidaiji is a thinly disguised relic of native customs and beliefs.

As in all Eastern agricultural communities, phallic worship
of one sort or another is very common. My friend Professor
Nishioka has written a book entitled *The History of
Phallicism in Japan*. Many of the phallic statues which were
quite a frequent sight in the rice fields have now been hidden
away. Nevertheless, one can still see them—strange stone
carvings jutting out among the rice stalks in the remoter

parts of the country. Even today one can see on Shoten Island in Ueno Park, in the center of Tokyo, a large explicitly phallic symbol in the shrine. From the front it is a hooded figure of a bearded man holding a staff, but from the side and back there is no doubt what it is meant to represent. The emphasis is sometimes greater. Nishioka in his book illustrates two banners at the Tagata shrine in Aichi prefecture with hideously realistic paintings of male organs on them. This shrine seems to go in for emblems of this sort, and Nishioka saw a large collection of wooden, china and stone phalli—one at least four feet long—at this shrine in 1954.

The fact that Japan was cut off for so long seems to have meant that the influence of the primitive religions has lingered on more forcibly than one would have expected. In some parts of the country one of the great rituals which surround the rice growing involves giving a bath to a double-ended radish, which is recognized as a fertility symbol.

The Japanese, whether from cause or effect I cannot say, are remarkably unconcerned in their approach to sex. A friend of mine was asked one day to what he was told was an ordinary business luncheon in Osaka. And certainly it appeared to be perfectly ordinary. He sat among fifty quiet-looking businessmen, all discussing their affairs quite naturally. Toward the end of lunch a man came in and said that the president of the company had invited him to exhibit a product which he thought might be of some use to members of the company. He said that it was a household gadget, which produced rather unexpected laughter from the other guests.

There was a dais at one end of the room and the man stood

on it and held up, for all to see, a mock penis. He then called in two girls, who undressed. He then attached the penis to one of them by means of a strap and they gave an exhibition of its usefulness. After the performance was over the man came around to each of the businessmen and sold a large number of these objects, assuring them that they need never worry again about keeping their wives happy. What surprised my friend almost more was that after dressing again the two girls came and sat down and drank tea with the guests, behaving with absolute decorum and apparently quite unembarrassed. He was struck also by the fact that the whole arrangement had been received without any sniggering or dubious jokes. If anything at all was expressed it was appreciation of the host's thoughtfulness.

Saidaiji, which appeared to me to have a rather lubricious atmosphere, was accepted equally by everyone there as perfectly natural. If they were struck by anything, it was not that the boys were naked but rather by their incredible stamina. Indeed Yamaguchi appeared quite puzzled by the fact that I felt that the festival had such a sexual emphasis, although on being pressed he was prepared to admit that it had been derived from some fertility rite.

CHAPTER TEN

THE ABBOT

A︎LMOST every week I would go to a particular Zen temple which lay in the northwest corner of Kyoto. The word temple is difficult to define. I have used it throughout this book in contradistinction to shrine—temples being Buddhist and shrines being Shinto. In some cases a large temple would be divided into a number of subtemples rather in the way that a university is divided into colleges. The one I visited belonged to a group called Daitokuji, numbering about twenty-three subtemples which form one of the main headquarters of the Rinzai sect of Zen Buddhism. The twenty-three temples are set in a compound covering roughly twenty-seven acres, and the house belonging to Kobori San, which we had looked at during our house hunting, is one of them.

Another is Shinjuan. This temple is one of the smaller ones but it is classified as a Japanese national treasure. To reach it you go through the main compound, past some large empty-looking wooden buildings, with vast sweeping roofs, which are used only on ceremonial occasions. The compound is dotted with pine trees, leaning at extravagant angles, and from the broad space little alleyways lead to the various subtemples. Down one is the high gateway, set in a plaster wall, of Shinjuan. The wooden gate is large and not all that different from the gate of an Oxford college. As often as not it is closed and you go in through a narrow door beside the gate. Once through, you are in a small enclosed garden. Ahead is another roofed wooden gateway—always closed. There are carefully pruned pine trees, little hedges and shrubs and carpets of moss. The moss is brushed every morning and any fallen pine needles picked up. The pine trees are combed and prinked two or three times a week. Every branch is supported and directed. They bear the same sort of relation to ordinary pine trees that poodles do to ordinary dogs. To the left is a crisscrossed sliding door leading into the back of the temple.

As you push it open a small bell rattles, but if no one hears this there is a larger green copper bell hanging on a chain and a hammer to strike it with. It has a deep tone. There is always an answer, either from the abbot or from the old woman who cooks or one of the student monks. They answer with a call protracted on one note and then ending abruptly on a higher one. Then you take off your shoes, and one of them comes. You bow four or five times, and if it is the old woman she will kneel on the floor saying a greeting over and over. There are two huge high steps to struggle up. Then you pass through a room with matting on the floor, and on a low stand a long oil painting of a battleship with bombs exploding around it. The donor gave some money as well. Out of there you see—beyond another small garden with a well— the central block of the temple. The huge roof, made of compressed chips of bark, has mellowed to a soft mossy brown.

The vast eaves sweep out and, at their corners, upward, projecting over the shining gray platforms of wood which run all around the building. The roof has to be renewed every twenty years at a cost of $15,000.

The rooms in the main building of the temple are big but dark. Their walls up to a height of about six feet consist only of sliding panels painted with faint landscape designs in black and white. Many of them are the work of Sesshu, one of Japan's best painters (1421-1507). On occasions these panels are taken out so that two or more rooms can be thrown together.

In the center of the building is a shrine (in the ordinary sense), totally dark as it is surrounded by the outer rooms. Above an altar sits a statue of the founder of the temple, Ikkyu (1394-1421), a famous Zen master. It is an ugly statue, made grisly by the fact that the hair and whiskers are Ikkyu's own. In front of the founder a table has on it offerings of fruit and sticky bean cakes.

To one side of the main block is another building, known as the princess' teahouse. The rooms here are low and bare except for sliding panels decorated this time with heavy gold and green and brown. At the back is the tearoom, so low that you have to bend double to get into it. This room is innocent of all decoration, relying on the pattern of the slat-like beams and on the light shining through the tiny squared paper windows to give it a Zen character. It is a wretched little foxhole, which always made me think of the inside of a miniature suburban garage, yet the Emperor and Empress nearly always come here for tea when they are in Kyoto. The main buildings and the teahouse are surrounded by about ten separate gardens, pampered but peaceful and beautiful, if barren to Western taste.

We encountered Sobin Yamada, the abbot of Shinjuan, fairly early on during our stay in Kyoto. The first time we went to see him we were taken by a friend who was living in a room in the princess' teahouse. He was an English student with very little money, and the abbot had agreed to put him up for a nominal rent of twenty dollars a month, which included all his food, such as it was. We arrived and went through the performance I have described of striking the bell and the elaborate greetings. It was the old woman who came to the door and she led us into the jumble of poky rooms near the entrance where she and the abbot and the student monks lived. There were only two students, for as a result of Westernization there is a scarcity of young men who want to enter the monastic life. But behind their rooms is an enormous hollow kitchen, evidence of the days, during the Tokugawa age, when monks were plentiful.

We sat on the floor in a small room with the paper screens open, looking on to the small garden with a well between the living quarters and the main block of the temple. There was no table—in fact nothing in the room except a scroll of calligraphy hanging in the *tokonoma* and, in the center of the floor, a large brazier made of china and half filled with powdery ash, on the top of which glowed a few sticks of charcoal. The matting in this room was worn and there were holes in the paper panes.

We sat for a while exchanging the normal pleasantries with the old woman, commenting on how hot it was, she expressing amazement at the fact that we had a child—the usual preamble which is the essential part of the first twenty minutes of any encounter. In a while the abbot came. He was dressed in a shantung silk kimono and an overkimono of black mesh nylon. Around his neck hung a band of black silk with two ivory rings at his waist. His head was closely shaved, and on his feet he wore only white *tabi* socks with divisions for the big toes. He was a short square man, but as soon as he came into the room one was aware of his dignity and strength. He looked only about thirty, but was in reality about eight years older. He took up a position near the brazier, kneeling on the floor beside a cushion. He bowed three or four times and as he rose between each bow he would suck in his breath with a sharp hiss and during his upright moments pronounce some formalized phrase. He did all this with extreme correctness, but as soon as it was over he started straight off with sensible questions and ordinary conversation. It is a curious thing that Zen monks, whose religion is responsible for much of the incoherence of the people, are themselves the most direct and forthright of their countrymen in ordinary everyday intercourse. Almost always with Zen monks one feels that immediate contact which one misses so drastically in nearly everyone else. Instantly he was smiling away as if he had known us all his life. Indeed he made no concessions to the fact that we were strangers, but kneeling down on the cushion he rocked to and fro, bending over until his face was almost in the brazier, barking rather abruptly at the old woman, his voice resounding on a hollow note as he spoke into the china bowl.

The old woman bustled about making tea. She fetched a small tea chest, a few battered-looking highly prized Korean

tea bowls, a small whisk made of bamboo and various paraphernalia. She made the abbot sit back while she put a kettle
on a trivet over the few sticks of charcoal, and we waited for
it to boil. These braziers are nearly always the only form of
heating in a Japanese house. If one piles the charcoal into
them one can get a glow which will take the chill off a very
small room, but normally there is in them only the very mini-
mum of fuel to keep them going, so that a room with only
paper screens to keep out the cold is hardly endurable. The
Japanese admit this but do very little about it. They just
content themselves with warming their hands and saying
over and over again, *"samui des' ne'* (it's cold)." The only
way of getting warm in winter is the bath.

It was summer now, and in time the kettle boiled. The
old woman then made the tea. Instead of the usual very weak
tea that one gets everywhere else, one is given in temples
the tea which is used in the tea ceremony. This is very thick,
sludgy stuff, made from a powder. It is vivid pea-green in
color, and to some virtually undrinkable. Martha never got
used to it, but in time I managed to get it down whenever we
were visiting the temple, in spite of the fact that it left in my
mouth a rather bitter taste which lasted for quite an hour.
The ritual was that a little of this stuff was poured into a
bowl and handed first of all to me. The abbot explained that
according to the correct etiquette I should hold up the bowl
and turn it around two and a half times before drinking.
This was to show my appreciation of the bowl itself. Strictly
speaking one should perform a rigmarole of bows at the same
time, but the abbot and I quite quickly gave up any pretense
that I would ever do it right. With the tea went a sticky cake

with brown bean paste in the middle covered over with a sort of rice glue. By the very end of my stay I found I could eat one of these during a visit of an hour and a half or so. Osho San, as Yamada would be more properly addressed, although he was pleased when one liked something, never took it in the least amiss if one refused it. That first day we sat talking for about two hours, lighting cigarettes from time to time, using a piece of charcoal picked out from the brazier with a pair of metal chopsticks. He told us all about his temple and his life there.

He was from the countryside, about forty miles from Kyoto, the son of a peasant farmer. He had come to Shinjuan when he was about fifteen as one of the student monks. Except for the war, his life has been almost precisely the same every day for twenty years. It is difficult to judge how much of his time is taken up in the straightforward practice of his religion. He performs a service in the chapel every morning at five o'clock and he spends hours in meditation from time to time, but these do not seem set or regular. The vast proportion of his day seems to be taken up in caring for the temple and the gardens. Every morning the great boards of the balconies are washed down by the abbot and his two students and the gardens are groomed with more care than any housewife gives to a room. While their actual living quarters are not particularly clean, are even threadbare, the rest of the temple and the gardens are spotless and perfect. This cleaning and tending of the buildings is obviously in itself something of a religious practice. It is hard to say where the line can be drawn between gardening for the sake of gardening, and gardening for the sake of a mixture of art and religion.

There are beautiful treasures in the temple which he guards jealously, bringing them out of the storehouse only once a year for an airing. There are pictures, some Chinese, others Japanese, scrolls, pieces of cloth, brocades and embroidery, a certain amount of china and a few rather indifferent statues. Osho San's appreciation of these is emotional. His classification of them knows only one yardstick—"one hundred and fifty years old," "two hundred and fifty years old," "four hundred years old." Everything falls into one of these three categories and, as often as not, he picks the wrong one.

In spite of the temple's being a national treasure he is absurdly possessive about these objects. He invited me to go and see them on the day that he had them out for the airing and when I arrived I found the whole place barred and bolted and it was only when I had been thoroughly identified that I was admitted. When I asked him why there was all this secrecy, for the temple was normally open to the public and anyone could ask to come in, he said, "Oh, we don't want everybody looking at them."

"But surely you get some grant from the Government, and it is only on one day a year that they can be seen. Wouldn't it be kinder to let people in who enjoy them?"

"Certainly not. They belong to the temple—why should everyone see them."

Osho San had a certain streak of arrogance, one which was usually evident only in his capacity as abbot of the temple. He ran the place with an absolute certainty that he knew what was best. He was quite severe with the old woman, Obā San—old woman—as she was known. She never used to eat with us. She always had her bath last, and by our standards he used her really like a servant, although as it happened she had some money of her own. His treatment of her was, of course, in part the normal attitude of any man to any woman, but it was also partly dictated by his position.

It was not easy to understand exactly how the affairs of the temple worked. Osho San had been the favorite protégé of the previous abbot, who had apparently just appointed him as his successor. This appointment had to have the rough approval of the head of the main temple in Daitokuji, but there seemed to be no particular need for qualifications other than being the abbot's favorite. Osho San said that he would choose his own successor and later he offered to adopt Sebastian, saying that he would bring him up to be the next abbot. When I refused, he seemed almost surprised, being satisfied with his life and considering it an enviable one. Certainly in some ways it is and interesting in that it is no different from that of his predecessors over three hundred and fifty years.

It is a life of absolute peace, cut off within the compound from everything to do with the outside world, and maintaining, as it is impossible to maintain in any other modern industrialized country, the atmosphere, entire and unaltered, of former centuries.

We came to know Osho San almost better than any other Japanese person we met during our stay. Oddly enough, we can be said to have altered his life quite considerably during the time that we were there. The segregated existence which he had led except for the few brief years of the war, during which he went to Manchuria, had made him curiously naïve and innocent. He was at the same time intensely proud of Japan and very conscious of all its traditions and customs. Very often as we were sitting having tea in the threadbare little room he would tell us about some place, or some custom and suggest that we go and see it. We would then persuade him to come too. As a result, particularly as communication was very difficult until we learned to speak some Japanese, our relationship was made up of expeditions of maple or moon viewing, or visits to special restaurants.

These outings were in their way rather bizarre. There would be ourselves, eager and interested to learn as much as possible; there would be old Obā San, desperately anxious to be left out of nothing; and Osho San himself, rather like a schoolboy on a treat, excited, proprietary and rather over-doing everything. He cannot have been rich, and what money he had came presumably from donations given to the temple, although the old woman supplemented this with the money left to her by her husband. Nevertheless, Osho San on our excursions was never satisfied with anything less than the best, in the same way that it would not have occurred to him to have anything other than a pure-silk kimono. He was always exasperated by anything that we took for granted, such as waiting for a streetcar. He would set out firmly announcing that No. 16 streetcar was the one we needed. When we got to the stop he would peer up and down the road asking impatiently when we thought it was going to arrive. Then, after at the most a minute and a half of grunting and questioning passers-by and complaining vociferously, he would hail a taxi. Usually, however, we had our car and this was a matter of great pleasure to him. He was always asking me how much it cost to run, and whether I thought it would be a good idea for him to buy one like it.

One of the first expeditions we made was a boat trip down the rapids of a river not far from Kyoto. We left the car at the small town of Arashiyama, where the boat trip would end, and took the train which ran up the gorge of the river. Journeys of this kind, however short, were always a great performance with Osho San. He would make an issue of choosing the right carriage and seeing that we got seats on the correct side of the train for seeing the view. This was achieved to his satisfaction. On arrival there was a walk of about a quarter of an hour to the river's edge, and it was only with difficulty that we persuaded him that a taxi was not necessary. At the landing stage a great deal of care went into the choosing of the right boat and the hiring of competent-looking oarsmen. The boats were quite large, and one could share them with other people, but the abbot dismissed this idea as monstrous. We set off down the river, at first slow and winding and then narrowing to fast-running rapids so that enormous strength and skill were required to guide the boats between the rocks and prevent it from capsizing. On our way down, Osho San lectured us about the trees on the bank, about the temples we passed, and told us stories connected with the river and the villages near it. Only on one point was he entirely submissive to convention. We had brought sandwiches with us and were on the lookout for somewhere to stop and eat them. At length we came to an island in the middle of the river where several other boats were drawn up, their occupants eating their lunch on a pebble beach. There was a photographer with his apparatus set up offering to take photographs of parties from the boats. We suggested that it would be nicer to go on a bit and find somewhere more peaceful—another island or a pleasanter stretch of bank. But no, Osho San wouldn't argue about this with the oarsman. In this he was entirely Japanese—this was where everyone had lunch, this was the place to have lunch, this was where we would have lunch. And so we did.

We sat too on the pebble beach incongruously drinking wine from exquisite cups which had been taken out of the temple storehouse especially for the occasion.

We arrived back at Arashiyama, where we had left our car, late in the afternoon. There we went to a pleasant, expensive inn looking over a branch of the river, had a bath, the men first and then the women, and dinner, all of which must have cost about fifteen dollars and all of which was handled by Osho San with the aplomb of a man of the world.

It was only as we were driving home that he told us that this was the first time he had made this expedition, and the first time that he had eaten in a restaurant of this sort for many years. The Japanese have a word—*hajimete*—which means "this is the first time" and it was a word that almost became a joke between us, so many things did he do for the first time in our company.

He also seemed to find in us a quality of absolution. Zen priests, strictly speaking, are not meant to eat meat, or even fish. There is a Zen tradition of drinking although Osho San implied that he was not ordinarily happy about it. But when he was with us, he used to do all these things quite freely.

"It is quite all right," he used to say, "to have anything, provided that one does not buy it for oneself. If it is offered one, it is plainly rude to refuse."

So there were many parties we had together at which he used to become quite excitable, but on the other hand he had a very much stronger head than most ordinary Japanese people, and I think it did him good. The food on the temple was so bad, so self-denying, that very often he was quite ill, plainly as a result of it.

One evening we went there for a special banquet which he laid on for us. We ate it in one of the large rooms of the temple not usually used. There was not even the comfort of a table, as in an inn, to provide some support to lean against while kneeling on the floor. Here one was supposed to kneel with one's heels under one, lift the bowl to one's mouth and feed oneself with chopsticks with the other hand—a peculiarly difficult feat. Anyhow, on this occasion there were about seventeen courses, none of them made with any prohibited article, each one more particularly repulsive than the last and, I should imagine, without a calorie between them.

Very often Osho San would be in bed in the afternoon when we called, and the old woman would say that he had had a dizzy spell while working in the garden. He was a strong man, and outwardly very healthy, and I am convinced that the cause of these spells was quite simply undernourishment.

One of the best *hajimete* evenings we had with the priest was the night he decided we should see a geisha girl. He did not tell us what he had arranged, but merely asked whether we would go with him to a restaurant where we could eat overlooking the river. In the summer in Kyoto the houses which overhang the water on the west bank of the river near the center of the town all become restaurants. Some are open all the year, but others wait just for this season. As soon as the rains are over, a throng of carpenters arrives and from the back of each of these houses a platform is thrown out on stilts above the narrow towpath. One of these belonged to some friend of Osho San's, a friend whom he said he had not seen for twenty years.

We were received with a mixture of infinite courtesy and enthusiasm. It was one of the few occasions when we went somewhere and were treated absolutely genuinely as ordinary people. That evening I realized that no matter where one went or what one did, how enthusiastic people seemed, there was always an intangible reserve in all relationships with foreigners impossible to break down in only a year. Mrs. Kazama, our landlady, Imamura of the seminar, and Osho San himself were probably the only people who accepted us entirely. The students, about whom I shall write in the next chapter, although I may have communicated with them better than with Osho San, always regarded me as something apart. And this evening, in the restaurant belonging to Osho San's friend, was the only occasion in a public place when I knew myself, without any question, to be accepted.

There were, that night, a lot of first times for Osho San. It was the first time he had been to his friend's restaurant. It was the first time he had eaten lobster. And it was the first time he had ever employed a geisha. In a burst of wild extravagance, he had told his friend the restaurant keeper to get a *maiko,* or apprentice geisha, for one hour. This must have cost him about twelve or fifteen dollars. He said nothing about her until she arrived. We were sitting out on the platform watching the sunset reflected in the shallow water of the nearly dried-up river bed. On either side of us were other platforms with parties going on, and at one of them was a pretty young *maiko.* As it happened I teased Osho San about this, saying it wasn't at all a suitable sight for a priest. So he was absolutely bubbling over with excitement at the thought of what he had done. The *maiko* from the next-door party disappeared, and five minutes later she arrived to entertain us.

All the girls come from a central pool, and it just happened that she had been booked for us just after the people at the next-door restaurant. It was fascinating to notice that when she arrived on our platform, which was not more than thirty feet away from the party where she had just been performing, she never made any sign or even glanced at the people she had just been with. Once we had hired her she was there to pay attention to us and not to anybody else.

She didn't seem the least bit taken aback at having to entertain a priest and, at the same time, she was determined to make the most of him as he was of her. Even the *maiko* seemed to forget that we were foreigners, for usually all they will do for tourists is to play idiotic games. But on this occasion I got a better impression of what a geisha party was like. But as I have said before, even the conversation of geishas seems to us pretty dull. She went on at the abbot, making jokes about his clothes—"Is that a nightgown you've got on?"

Osho San's replies were rather better than hers, I thought, as he looked her up and down and brought out finally, "Mine may look like a nightgown, but isn't, whereas yours doesn't look like one."

As usual, Osho San managed to make it appear that he had spent all his life bantering with geisha girls. As always he was overgenerous and insisted on the girl's having a meal at his expense—not with us for they never eat in public—when she had finished dancing. I really began to feel that if we had stayed too long in Kyoto, the temple funds would have dwindled to nothing.

There were simpler, less expensive outings. There was the evening when we went cormorant fishing, another *hajimete* for Osho San, though again he did not admit it until afterward. This also took place at Arashiyama and this time we took Osho San to the same inn. After dinner we hired a boat—a lovely, rough, wooden boat with a flat bottom and a high prow at each end. On the floor was matting, and over our heads a canopy of wood like an old four-poster bed. The atmosphere was a little like what one imagines Victorian boating parties to have been, with considerably more license. There were some hundred or more boats, each with lighted paper lanterns hanging from them, moving haphazardly about, up and down the half-mile stretch of water where the fishing takes place. Nearly everyone was a little drunk, but not unpleasantly so. They all sang, and in some boats there were *maikos* playing *samisens*.

Osho San was wild with pleasure, stopping the boatmen every so often in order to buy from other passing boats packets of peanuts or their Japanese equivalent; cones of not-too-frozen ice cream, which goes in Japan under the name of *sofuto;* or fireworks, especially sparklers, which he waved around his shaved head with great flourish. It was some time before we finally came across the fishermen. They were in a boat about twice the size of ours, manned by three men. On the gunwale sat twelve cormorants angrily jostling one another for pride of place like a lot of old ladies in line at a surgery, though in fact each bird had its appointed place which never varied. Around their necks were strings attaching them like puppets to their masters. Fastened at right angles to the high front prow of the ship was a beam, and from its end about six feet above the water hung a basket filled with glowing sticks. At a given moment all the birds would be pushed or would jump over the side into the water, where they would splay out like geese flying in formation. They fished mostly in shallow water, and as soon as the birds were beneath the surface one could see them in the light of the fire somehow quite changed from one's usual conception of a bird. All at once they were like snakes, streaming through the water, evil in shape and primitive. The boat itself made a fine sight, high prowed and unchanged in shape for hundreds of years, worked by three figures with bright cotton bands around their heads, their clothes, too, the same for centuries. And, perhaps, prettiest of all, a fearful stream of confetti falling from the fire—not just ash, but an unending plethora of moths, tempted by the flame and falling behind in a steady white wake. Then a pause—the birds would surface and be dragged back on to the boat again and there made to disgorge their catch.

The cormorants would then rest awhile, jostling once again

on the gunwale, preening their feathers, their birdlike quality restored. We went over to the fishing boat in one of these intervals in the birds' work. One of us got over the side of our boat in the shallow water and went to examine the cormorants. The fishermen gave a shriek of warning and told us that we mustn't on any account go near the birds. They have apparently an unexpected ferocity and, in spite of being trained and tamed in a sense, they hate anyone but their master coming near them. They lash out, pecking viciously at the eyes of strangers who approach too close, and the fishermen told us that it is quite a common thing to be blinded by them. The fishermen themselves came from a prefecture about eighty miles from Kyoto. There are only two or three places where cormorant fishing is practiced, and these men move from one to another according to the season. It is not particularly profitable but it makes for them a reasonable living, for each bird is capable of catching as many as six fish at one time and may well dive for two or three hours an evening. The cormorants require considerable training, but on the other hand can be worked for something like fifteen years, and a good bird about six years old is sometimes worth $300.

The whole scene in the delicious evening setting of Arashiyama was particularly delightful—the broad river, alive with floating lights; on one bank gay restaurants with kimonoed men sitting on balconies eating and drinking, and the other bank rising steeply to the wooded hillsides, dark and overhanging. With Osho San sitting bolt upright on the floor of the boat, excited and voluble, we felt somehow as though we were capturing something of the real spirit of the country, a false illusion, probably, but one which we often got on these expeditions with the Zen priest.

I remember one evening with him—the night before one of the two big festivals in Kyoto, when the whole town turned out to see the palanquins which were to be drawn through the streets in procession the following day. I remember it not particularly because it was with Osho San, but more because it was the only occasion when I witnessed any act of violence or cruelty. The streets were packed so tight that it was impossible to move except with the crowd. The usual noise of the traffic was gone, for cars were banned that evening. The only sounds were those of many thousand wooden clogs shuffling over the tarmac, and the loudspeakers directing the crowds using incongruously polite forms of Japanese: "Would Mr. Everybody kindly keep to the left."

To get out of the crowd we turned down a narrow market street, hardly more than a passage, with food shops on either side, their wares overspilling from the stores until only a path ahead of us, there was a loud shouting and disturbance. A man in an undershirt had grabbed a tangerine off a pile in front of one shop. The shopkeeper tore out after him and the crowd, which was thick enough even in this side street, pounced on the man, dragging him to the ground, where he lay still and waiting. There was a brief pause, then, as at a signal, the crowd around him started kicking savagely and brutally. For a moment he lay inert, accepting it, until the pain of the flailing clogs tore into his flesh. He started to scream. His voice was like that of a *kabuki* actor, high pitched and unreal. He yelled long and agonizingly. The more he shrieked the more they kicked. After nearly a minute of this he leaped wildly to his feet and, thrusting through the crowd, ran off. There was nothing I could do in the face of this fierce determined crowd, set on their violent vengeance, but it was all over as abruptly as it had started.

The men who had been kicking him, when they saw me, composed their faces again and bowed sheepishly to the shopkeeper and went away. Osho San did not seem at all put out by this. Like the rest of the Japanese people he had no liking for the police and thought it a swifter, simpler solution than calling in the law to deal with the matter. It was, as I say, the only occasion on which I saw anything in the behavior of the people which might correspond, even remotely, with the wartime brutalities which are such a problem for the visitor to equate with the friendly behavior and attitude of the people he comes across.

As a rule I found it difficult to talk to Osho San about his religion and he was such a perfect example of someone who lived rather than discussed his beliefs that I never saw much point in it. He was not a philosopher, nor was he a saint. It was, I thought, easier to forget his calling. However, when Arthur Koestler came for his visit to the country, I tried for his sake to get at something of the motivations which made Osho San choose his way of life. The language barrier at this level of discussion proved too much, so Osho San arranged that Arthur and I should, through interpreters, talk to the heads of his temple, so that Arthur might find out something of the views of the ordinary practicing Zen monks as well as of the philosophers and experts with whom he had been discussing the development of Buddhism in Japan. He will write of these discussions in a more proper context than I can attempt, but there was one meeting with Arthur and these priests that I feel is interesting if only for the atmosphere in which it was conducted.

We had been the day before to see the administrator of the temple and had not got very far owing to having a rather poor interpreter. But on this morning we were to meet the head abbot. His temple was not far from Shinjuan, but in spite of being that of the chief priest, it was not a particularly interesting building, excepting for the hall where the monks practiced their rigorous eighteen-hour meditations, during which they are beaten with a stick if their thoughts stray from the matter in hand. We were shown into a very large room. Along one wall were a row of cushions for us to kneel on. We took up our positions on these cushions facing the *tokonoma,* in front of which was placed an enormous red and blue cushion twice the size of ours. For some time we waited. At length the chief abbot came in, a surprisingly large, burly man without a trace of asceticism in his appearance. He was accompanied by a strikingly beautiful, spare, taut monk whose presence I had often admired when I had seen him about the compound. But in spite of the chief priest's worldly look he was determined to exact all the deference to which his office entitled him. We bowed very low, and he bowed to each of us in turn, and then he knelt on his enviably thick cushion while we got on to our rather thin ones. After a while, in the manner of royalty, he gave us permission to sit on them without our heels under us. Tea was brought for us in rather drab cups, and for him in a wonderfully designed one, plainly Chinese, covered in red and green dragons. This had a lid to keep the tea warm. We had minute braziers beside each of us, barely warm enough to light a cigarette had we dared to.

It became plain very early on that he was not going to answer any of the questions which Arthur put to him. He was doggedly determined to be obstinate, and if he felt we were trying to pin him down he would then nod to the superb-looking monk and tell him to answer. We started off with perfectly simple, direct questions.

"Is there," we asked, "a metaphysic in Zen?"

"No."

"Is there judgment between good and evil?"

"None."

"Why then is Zen not immoral?"

"By Zen you cross into a world where good, evil and beauty do not exist, and having seen this, you are free to come back to this world and see that they do not exist here either."

"Is it evil to kill?"

"It is bad to kill in peace, but good in war. If a mosquito bothers you, you must not kill it, but you must chase it."

To almost every question they would answer with an inconsequential parable:

"A horse in Tokyo eats," a monk would say, "and a horse in Osaka feels full."

"But that is totally meaningless."

"It is no more unreasonable than when a Sputnik goes up in Russia and the stocks go down in New York."

Arthur was as good as they were at their own game.

They produced parables—Arthur would think up one of his own.

"A man is on his way to prayer," Arthur would start (transposing the problem of guilt by omission raised in Camus' *La Chute*). "He is crossing an elegant red lacquer bridge," he continued with the irrelevant elaboration with which they always peppered their stories. "From beneath the bridge comes a cry from the still, deep water. The Zen monk is so intent upon his prayer that he does not hear the cry for help."

In the same way that they always answered logic with parables, they answered parables with logic. "But he would hear, and he should go to him," they answered, half admitting that Arthur had put a pertinent question.

I had a mild exchange on the question as to whether Zen was a religion for everyone.

"We press nobody," the chief priest answered. "If I decided to go to Tokyo I do not insist that everyone should accompany me."

Applying Arthur's tactics I said, "A man is living in poverty. In tending his aged mother and mixing her medicines his discovers the panacea for all ills. Should he cure only his mother?"

The chief priest looked furious. "Zen is open to everyone to find for himself,"—another logical answer.

The interview was plainly not going well, so I closed the subject and tried to get the answers to a few straightforward questions about the method of support for the whole temple, which was my main concern and about which Osho San had always been very vague. They answered a few of them with lies. They professed to live on not more than six dollars a month each, which I knew was both impossible and untrue. They declared that they had no government help, which was also inaccurate, as many of the buildings which are national treasures are maintained in part by government funds—and having delivered himself of this typically Zen remark: "We live by mendicancy—two or three of us go out into the street, but we don't beg, we happen to have a bowl in our hands into which people happen to put money." The chief priest stood up and declared, "Your logical questions merely embarrass us."

There are, as it happens, if one studies Zen, adequate answers to all the simpler questions which we put—answers which do not conflict with logic. One delightful philosopher by the name of Nishitani answered all of them for me in the course of ten minutes' pleasant conversation. There are, he told me, basic moral commandments in Buddhism, but Zen is concerned with what is beyond social morality in the same way that Christian love is beyond ethics. Zen has in it the danger of the sin of omission, but there was one Zen master who said, "Do not go to the other shore until all others have reached it." Nishitani further explained that the Japanese had adopted the Confucian code in much the same way that Christianity adopted Judaic law. But these questions are not within the scope of this book, and I mention them only in order to dispel any idea that my account of this interview is written in a spirit of mockery of Zen. It is only meant to show how all-pervasive is the Japanese preference for the indefinite.[1]

---

[1] I have also considered whether they were simply taking us for a ride. I think not and Arthur Koestler's opinion is that if it was a ride, it was what he calls "the orthodox ride—the ride they take themselves for." His account of this interview can be read in *The Lotus and the Robot,* The MacMillan Co., 1961.

This Zen preference is, incidentally, noticeable also in Shinto, the original religion of Japan. Broadly speaking, the practice of Shinto consists in praying to the *kami*—undefined spirits who in turn pass the prayer on to another spirit. No one can say with any precision what the spirits are or what they represent. The emphasis in Shinto lies in *what* you do. Why you do it may be unexplained. Shinto festivals involve taking the spirit of one shrine out for an airing—moving a palanquin from one place to another and then returning it. If you ask the priest why this is done he will not answer. The secrets of his office lie in knowing precisely how it is done.

A girl once said to me "It does not matter why. In the Tokugawa age we learned to keep everything to ourselves. What counts is what we feel inside our breast, so we do not want to have a dogma."

Even this was fanciful, for Shinto was undogmatic long before the Tokugawa age.

The other sects of Buddhism have a dogma, often a rich one, but it is my feeling that Zen's lack of it has had a perceptible influence on the culture of Japan.

CHAPTER ELEVEN

THE STUDENTS

THE Japanese have a passion for learning, almost a morbid desire for knowledge. As soon as it got about that there was an Englishman living in the quarter where we had found our house, I was constantly besieged with requests to teach English. On one occasion I remember a pair of young builders coming to the door and asking if they could study with me. I agreed but when it come to the matter of fees I made a great mistake. I felt that I would get as much out of it as they would and I realized they were probably only earning about thirty dollars a month, so I said I would teach them free. At once the conversation became rather chilly, and they left saying that they would get in touch with me. They never did. I was told later that I had probably upset them on two counts. First of all I would be putting them under an intolerable obligation and, secondly, what sort of a teacher could I be if I did not want any money for it? So when, soon after, I was approached by a small group of students I was more cautious. Again I was worried about taking money from them because students are pathetically poor in Japan and often have to take jobs for long hours at night in order to pay their university fees. I said that I would teach them if they

228

would undertake to keep me supplied with beer and, as the evenings on which they came were practically the only occasions on which I drank beer, it seemed to work out quite adequately.

I taught them over a period of about six months and during that time their number varied, so that there were only three who came consistently throughout the time. Two of these were young men—one an undergraduate called Inoue, the other a postgraduate, Ozaki. The other regular was a girl called Satsuko Ito. They were, I think, fairly typical of the mass of Japanese students. A university degree is almost essential if a young person is going to get any sort of job worth having. This is slightly less forbidding than it sounds, for there are nearly five hundred universities in the country, the standard of most of which is dismally low. This small group of people was especially interesting to me because presumably it was they who were to shape the destiny of Japan.

It is a little hard to describe the atmosphere of those evenings on which they used to come, for the attitude of Japanese students is so far removed from any accepted ideas one may have about the ways of youth that one had to use an entirely different approach. They would arrive at the door, never using the bell as one might have expected, but instead talking rather loudly on the doorstep until my attention was attracted.

No Japanese ever uses the bell. The tradesmen push the door open and yell "good morning" with a curious guttural emphasis on the last syllable, or bellow one's name in the same way, and then just stride in. Older, more formal, callers stand outside the door bleating "good afternoon" rapidly until one comes. By some curious chance there was a smudge on the notice which we had put in Japanese just outside the door which asked callers to ring once for us and twice for the people in the flat above, and this smudge apparently made it read that they should ring fourteen times for us and twenty-four for the upstairs flat. It was typical of life in Japan that the few people who did ring the bell resignedly followed these instructions down to the last ring.

The students were the shyest of all and, if I was busy doing something, I might not realize for ten minutes that they were there. They would wait patiently until I came, but eventually I taught them to use the bell. They would come in, take off their shoes and troop into the sitting room in Indian file, bowing repeatedly. "How are you these days?" they would ask each week, no matter how often I told them that this was a greeting rather sparingly used in English. Then, after some nervous discussion over where they should sit, they each sat in the same place each week.

Miss Ito would keep her feet very close together and sit bolt upright, her back never touching her chair. She was a pretty girl, with the flat broad face one associates with carvings of Kannon. She was always beautifully dressed but her clothes were rather young for her age. Often she wore what was really a schoolgirl's jumper, made of quite pretty material, over a fawn sweater. Her voice was very soft, sinking often almost to a whisper. She spoke rather slowly with a mildly arch formality. Her hands she would clasp in her lap and for the whole evening they would remain quite rigid, clenching and whitening whenever she talked. It was some months before I could get her to lean back comfortably.

She was at the time a Protestant but has, I am told, since embraced the Catholic faith on the grounds that a middle-aged parson proposed marriage to a young friend of hers. Slender grounds for a change of faith emphasizing once again the unimportance, for the Japanese, of a dogma in religious matters.

Ozaki was about twenty-eight and, as is quite common among students, reluctant to plunge out into the world, pre-ferring to go on and on with his studies, with the rather vague hope of becoming a professor. His English was the best and often he could write it with hardly a mistake, but as they are inclined to learn English rather in the way that we learn Latin, their performance in speech is nearly always way behind their written ability. He was usually the spokes-man for the class, and was undoubtedly the most intelligent. He was correspondingly the most afraid of making mistakes. As soon as he sat down he would take from his pocket a handkerchief and throughout the evening he would knead it in his hands, twisting and pulling at it ceaselessly and, after speaking, he would each time mop his face.

Inoue was quite different from the others. He seemed at first sight more composed. He sat with incredible stillness. He also never relaxed in his chair, but would lean forward resting his elbows on his knees and stare at me throughout the evening fixedly and with such rapt attention that at first I was quite disconcerted. His face was long and thin, and, apart from his shock of hair which seemed to know of no control, it was the long white face of the woodblock print. His nose was very straight, his mouth finely cut, but his eyes were the chief feature of his face—or perhaps they merely seemed so because they were always riveted on me. He wore usually the Prussian uniform of the schoolboys and students which made his appearance even more set. But certainly one could see the stylized beauty, which the artists of the eighteenth and nineteenth centuries admired, perpetuated in this boy's face. Some evenings he never spoke but remained silent and staring the whole time. On the few occasions that he did utter, it was in a low urgent voice, very fast and troubled. It may be that he was the most tortured of the lot.

Their attitude toward me was inevitably colored by the respect due to a teacher. This is a hard and fast, ingrained precept—that the teacher's word is indisputable and that the teacher himself is an elevated person. The Japanese word for any form of instructor, doctor, or even sometimes author, is *sensei.* I found that even in remote villages, if one were introduced as being a *sensei,* it caused a considerable impression even on maids in an inn. The duty owed to a teacher can be almost crippling, for it is unending—anyhow during the teacher's lifetime. There are cases of men of sixty who have made interesting discoveries in their field but are unable to publish them because they would contradict the teaching of some old master under whom they had studied when young, that old master being still alive, albeit aged ninety and past noticing anything. It would be an affront to publish anything which conflicted with what he had said forty years before. Teachers quite often trade on this, aided and abetted by others. I have, for example, a young friend of thirty who had assisted his teacher in translating some novel into Japanese. He had been set by the teacher to translate three more, all of which were published with his teacher's name on the title page, no reference being made to my friend. The publishers would not consider taking a book translated by the boy on his own initiative until he had done at least another one for his teacher without any credit—and then only if the teacher gave his consent.

So around me, for these students, there was this aura of sanctity. I felt in all of them the same search for a parent figure which had been so strong in the young boy who worked in the *kabuki* bar. Even up to the very end it was as much as I could do ever to get them to disagree with me. Inoue one day brought me a book.

"I would like you to read this book," he said in his jerky fashion. "It is a very good book."

I thanked him for it, but had to tell him that I had already read it and, on the whole, I thought it wasn't a very good book for various reasons.

He took it back from me saying "I will read it again."

I don't know whether he did or not but back he came the next week beaming with delight and, before he had even sat down, he said, "I have read the book again. You are right, it is a very bad book."

He was absolutely amazed at my explosion.

"Why in heaven's name can't you come back and say that you disagree with me—that you have read it again and that you still like it."

He could not see that we might get nearer to finding out whether the book was good or bad if we were to discuss it, each from his own standpoint. It was enough for him that I didn't like it.

The essays and theses which the students had to write at their university were themselves a clue to this question of opinions. They used to bring them to me for correction. The object was that I should merely help them to get their English right and I used to try not to get involved with the subject matter of the essays. Every so often it was almost more than I could bear. They managed to transport even into the English language their native vagueness, although philologically it was interesting that they couldn't achieve quite such masterpieces of indefinition in a foreign tongue. They overcame this by prefacing almost every paragraph with the words "it is said," "some say," or "many may think." I remember a particular essay of Miss Ito's. It was liberally peppered with phrases of this sort.

"It is said that Keats was a most romantic poet, and many may think that he was perhaps as good as Shelley, or that Shelley was as good as Keats."

"Which do you think is better, Keats or Shelley?" I asked.

"I think I like Keats best."

"Well, why in heaven's name don't you say so? Why not start your sentence with the statement: 'Keats was, in my opinion, the best of the romantic poets'?"

She looked scandalized and when I begged her to come out with some opinion, some personality, she told me that the teacher would not like it. Her teacher had said that students had no business to have opinions, they were there to learn what the teachers told them. If the teacher liked Shelley, they must like Shelley, and there was an end of it.

It is perhaps a little overfanciful to attribute to a succession of teachers, each holding different opinions, the fact that the other major difficulty I had with the students was to arouse even the faintest spark of interest in presenting their comments in any logical sequence. It never seemed to cross their minds that if one thing was so, another must follow. I remember another essay of Miss Ito's, entitled: "Why I study English." Roughly speaking, it went like this:

"I study English because I like poetry. The first English poem I read was 'An Ode to a Nightingale' by John Keats. I remember I was a little girl of ten, lying in bed when I read this poem, which is said to be one of his most beautiful. The other English poems which I liked are such and such. I like poetry better than prose because I am very fond of Japanese *haiku*."

I pointed out that nowhere in this sequence of thought had she really said why she liked English. She didn't say that England had produced the best poetry, or more poetry, which might account for her first sentence. If one could draw any conclusion it was that she liked Japanese poetry. I argued with her about this for about half an hour, but I got nowhere.

Another student brought me, on another occasion, an essay entitled: "Shakespeare and Jane Austen." This started out badly enough, "It is said that Jane Austen is very like Shakespeare." This was at the stage when my bias about not interfering with the subject matter was still strong, so I made no comment.

"I will now show why," was his next sentence. There followed a detailed account of the plot of *Pride and Prejudice*, at the end of which the essay petered out. The first sentence was the only one in which Shakespeare was mentioned.

This question of logic has side effects beyond the picturesque—ones which make one alarmed for the future of Japan. There was introduced into the Diet a bill widening the powers of the police, giving them rights of arrest and search which had an uncomfortably reminiscent flavor of the pre-war authoritarian state. The students were about evenly divided as to the merits of the bill when I raised the question one evening. The bill had been announced a couple of days before and, while details of the clauses had been published in the vernacular press, they had not as yet been printed in full in the English-language newspapers. I was therefore hazy about the exact points of principle involved. The students became unusually heated on the subject, getting almost more indignant with one another than I had ever seen Japanese people get in public. So, after about a quarter of an hour of this, I thought it would be as well to get it absolutely straight as to what we were arguing about and asked them to tell me the precise issues involved. Not one of them could do so. They had all read the leading articles—by nature rhetorical and inexact—but not one of them had read the actual bill itself, even though it had appeared on the same pages. I asked them how on earth they could discuss the thing properly. Those of them who supported the bill said that they were Conservatives and therefore it must be right. Those who opposed it said that they were Socialists and it must be wrong.

Here was an echo of what Imamura at the seminar had told me—give them a slogan and they would shout it senselessly. Here was the blind obedience to authority. Here was the same embarrassment at logic which the Zen priests had expressed. For all their professed love of democracy they were not really concerned with it. They were concerned with binding themselves to a teacher, to a master, perhaps one day again to an emperor.

Even in these young people, who claimed to admire England above all other countries, there was a suppressed longing to return to the old ways of Japan—not necessarily the immediate pre-war days, but to the days when everything was ordered and laid down, when everyone had his station, when everyone knew how to behave in any given situation. It may be unjust to say that it was a longing, it may have been an inability to escape from the past. Certainly they seemed to me unusually preoccupied with their country's traditions and customs. Left to themselves to choose the subject for an essay they would always pick something like "The History of the Tokaido Road," or "The Drinking Customs of the Japanese." This may have been a manifestation of the desire to do what they thought I would want. But, if so, it was carried to a degree so absurd as really to amount to a different aspect of the same problem. Even though they professed to be modern they were almost as constricted by the web of obligation as their parents had been. They were just as frightened of being conspicuous.

There was one evening when Ozaki made a mistake. I wanted to know the name of a hotel in a town called Kinosaki. I thought I had it written on a piece of paper in Japanese, and pointed to the characters in question asking him to read them for me.

"Ah, the Shirosaki Hotel," he said.

The others all laughed. In fact what I had got written down was the name of the town, Kinosaki, which can also be read—though in this case it never is—as Shirosaki. Ozaki blushed, and then laughed twice as loudly as anybody else and talked feverishly for about half an hour flat out.

Some weeks later he wrote something for me and in the

essay mentioned the incident, saying "However long I live, I shall never forget the laughter of my fellow students when I made a mistake in reading the character for Kino as Shiro." Who can imagine a world so harshly circumscribed that a man of twenty-eight can still feel that he will remember such a trivial mistake for the rest of his life?

The fear of being laughed at is a grave preoccupation in Japan. My lack of understanding of this I now realize is an explanation of another evening with the students when we were discussing the differences in sense of humor between the East and the West. I had been reading a book on Japanese humor with a mounting sense of inadequacy. I tried out one of the stories on the students in order to learn why they thought this was funny. The story was written in that peculiar Japanese style which includes a great number of irrelevancies. It was about Bishop Somebody-or-other who was the brother-in-law of somebody else who never appeared in the story again. This bishop had outside his house an enormous nettle tree, and he was consequently nicknamed Bishop Nettle. When I got to this point of the story the students began to laugh. The bishop was put out at this nickname so he cut down the tree, and was thereafter called Bishop Tree-stump. At this point the students dissolved helplessly. The bishop was made even angrier at this nickname, so at great labor he had the tree stump dug up, leaving a large hole in the ground, which filled with water. After this he was known as Bishop Dug-out-pond. I have never had a greater success with a story. The students were rolling about and it was quite ten minutes before I could get them to make an attempt at enough sense to explain what they thought was funny about it.

"But don't you see the frustration of the man? And the absurdity of his vanity? Nothing he did could help him to escape from being called by a nickname."

"Yes, I can see about the vanity, but really there must be crisper ways of pointing out the foolishness of vanity."

It was only afterwards that I realized what must have been comic to them. It was the inescapable, never-ending vista of the bishop being laughed at.

They were kind, the students—kind and trusting—and in half a way I felt that I was creating real friendships with them. But at the same time I sensed that I was never really going to get through to them, although our lives met for a long time at a peripheral level and that if later we continued to correspond, it would be a ritual rather than a mark of real affection. The gap was too broad to be bridged fundamentally.

It was a feeling that pervaded the whole experience of Japan. If one sat down next to somebody at dinner, there was never that instantaneous meeting which can come to you in any other part of the world. It seemed that the whole nation was determined to preserve its privacy and that each individual was determined never to get involved with another. It was true not only of my relationship with the students, but even of the students with one another. They never got, even after six months, on to the same sort of terms which a group of English students would have reached among themselves in only a couple of meetings. It is my impression, agreed with by some Japanese I know, that Japanese people simply do not have the same number of friends that Westerners do. Moku Yanagawa had about two men friends with whom he felt absolutely at ease. The others were merely companions, with whom he always preserved some sort of dignity and restraint. This may in part be due to the fact that there is no physical privacy in Japan. One young student explained to me that the mere fact of living in a Japanese house means that everything you do is known to somebody. It is almost unheard of to sleep alone; the families are large, so that one is seldom by oneself in a room and, even if one is, the walls are so thin as to separate one from a neighbor by only two sheets of paper, or at the most, half an inch of plaster. This, the student told me, made him avoid expressing on his face any feeling, for fear that somebody else would observe it. In the end this leads to the bottling up of emotions, to an unwillingness to reveal anything to anybody. It may perhaps account for some of the excessive nervousness which plagues all of them.

The burden of obligation, too, is so vivid a factor in everyone's life that it produces an even stronger caution in dealings with other people. The whole of social life is so carefully arranged that the living of it entails an effort which precludes the easy establishment of genuine understanding. One is constantly reminded of the circling and sniffing of two dogs meeting in the street. For me, obviously, living was more difficult. We are accustomed to look for an independence in relationships that we can admire—they are more satisfied with uniformity; we naturally search for stimulation—they endeavor to soothe; we care about the individual—they care about the group; we strive after adventure—they seek refuge in formality.

CHAPTER TWELVE

THE POLITICIANS

To go to the Diet, the Houses of Parliament, is a bizarre experience. It is probably one of the most erratic democratic chambers in the world. Fists fly with monotonous regularity, and a few visits to the Diet soon dispel any illusions of Oriental impassivity.

The political situation in Japan is typical of the whole of Southeast Asia. The parties, unlike those in the West, which slide together so as to become almost indistinguishable, diverge more and more and grow increasingly extremist. Democracy is a word, a slogan, another of those precepts to which the Japanese attach themselves with very little consideration as to its meaning. It is in this field that one becomes strongly aware more than in any other of the dichotomy of Japanese life and of the perennial ability of Japan to receive what is imposed upon it and adapt it to its own ways.

At first sight one is amazed to see that the Americans could have created a whole new system of government which has on the face of it been accepted. After a while one is conscious that, in spite of the outward satisfaction with the new system, there is a considerable element among the Conservatives

241

of yearning for the old security of surrendering everything to an absolute authority. The thing which gives me hope that the present situation is still fluid, that a transition from one state to another may still be achieved, is the fact that Japan has not gone Communist. There can never have been a people more perfectly the raw material for Communism. There is the age-old tradition of the importance of the community; there is the deeply seated respect for authority, there is the innate belief in the unimportance of the individual, and above all there is the total lack of that privacy which must be one of the greatest factors which prevents Europe from accepting Communism.

There is, in Nara prefecture, a village known as Shinkyo Buraku—Frame of Mind Village. Nineteen families live there in ideal communist style. Nothing is privately owned, not even underclothes or toothbrushes. The families work for the common good, farming, charcoal-burning and making *tatami*. They bathe together and eat together, though each family has its own room for sleeping. Anyone marrying into the village must give up all his possessions.

In spite of all these facts Communism has failed in Japan— even the villagers of Shinkyo Buraku vote Conservative.

The Conservative Party is at present soundly established. Even the most optimistic Socialist agrees that it will be at least ten years before there is any hope of his party being returned to power. It is no part of the purpose of this book to examine the political future of Japan, but Japan lies in the Pacific Ocean, America's one bastion against Red China, and one cannot help wondering what will happen to this country, almost the last of the Asiatic nations, excepting India, which has not yet abandoned the democratic form of government which the West has tried to impose on them. Japan still preserves the image, but it teeters on the edge.

The Conservative Government grows yearly more right wing; little by little chipping away at the constitution which MacArthur prepared for them. In the year that I was there the army, which Japan had sworn she would never again have, swelled its numbers, and is now a far cry from the self-defense forces which were the thin end of the wedge. The Police Bill was introduced, aimed at increasing the powers of the police. The Bill was shelved, but it is by no means forgotten. Another Bill was introduced to supervise the teachers to the point where the Ministry of Education would govern the teaching of morals in all schools. There were murmurs even of a movement to restore some of the power of the Emperor. The opposition to all these movements is great but the power of the Conservative Party may be greater still. It is their certain purpose to make it greater, to ensure that they remain in office and that the Socialist Party shall become an opposition only in name.

The Conservatives have also an advantage which could be equated with the use of the cross as their symbol by the Italian Christian-Democrat party. The Japanese character inclines them to favor conservatism. Perhaps even stronger than this—the Conservatives are in power, they represent authority. Being in power they are successful. Being in authority they have the respect of the nation, which believes in authority.

I did not meet many politicians, but I remember two in particular who seemed to represent well enough the parties to which they beyonged.

The first was Okada, the Foreign Secretary in the Labor

Shadow Cabinet. He was a jovial, fat man, lacking—as most politicians do—the natural nervousness of his countrymen. He was sporting enough to wear a buttonhole, but even in his *bonhomie* one could detect a despair natural in a man who was unlikely ever to realize his ambition. I sat with him for the whole of one morning in a club which was a sad imitation of a dull London club. It happened that it was the day after the Crown Prince's wedding and so he was preoccupied with the question of the Emperor and the status of the Imperial family.

"I have no feelings about them particularly," he said, "but as I watched yesterday's ceremony I could not help thinking that I was looking at something which had no reality. I do not approve of monarchy, it is quite out of date, and within the next few years I expect to see the natural extinction of the Emperor system. If they dabble in politics it will be quick. If not it may be slow, but then it doesn't matter. Anyhow, there will be no need for us to use force."

The wedding produced a curious phenomenon. An amnesty had been declared for violators of the election laws, a general election having been held in the previous summer. I had been slightly startled because the amnesty had meant a free pardon for eleven thousand people either in jail or awaiting appeal. I asked Okada if he didn't think this rather a lot of people to have infringed the election laws.

"Oh, not very many," he said. "The law is very strict and we catch all the little ones. But the big fish escape."

I asked him, if the Socialists were returned to power would they do anything to stamp out the corruption in Japan?

Corruption is extremely common, and politicians are generally assumed to be in the business for what they can make out of it. The papers, almost every day, carry some story about the bribery of officials or the general use of public funds for the wrong purposes. Political donations from corporations or private individuals are regarded as perfectly normal. Questions were asked in the Diet about a villa which the Prime Minister had built at a seaside resort. The questions were so phrased to imply that Premier Kishi had been helping himself to public money. A newspaper account at the time read as follows:

Prime Minister Nobosuke Kishi, while the Tory intra-party feud was at its highest, completed his gorgeous villa at Atami.

The completion of his house, plus the two hundred meter new road leading to his villa, came at a most inopportune time while he was under fire for his statement calling upon "money and power politics."

Opposition groups smell something fishy about this villa since considering his annual income as reported to the taxation office he can hardly build such a swanky house.

Kishi flatly denies foul play.

"The house was a present given by a certain firm as a token of gratitude for his 'small good offices'," he said.

The company identified as "K," incidentally, is reported to be playing a significant part in the Japan-Indonesia reparations programme.

This was quite all right. For "good offices" the Prime Minister can be rewarded with a villa and nobody complains. Even Okada was not very shocked at the thought of this.

"You do not understand Eastern politeness," he told me. "If somebody has done something to help you, even if it was his natural decision, one he would have made without any prompting, you must give him a present. There is no harm in that. If we came into power we would try to stamp out bribery, buying votes and that kind of thing. But we would not go against the traditional politeness of the Orient."

Corruption is common enough in the West—one has only to think of the United States or France—but when one considers that in each of the countries in Asia where there has been a military *coup* one of the main reasons given for the drastic step of revolution has been the need to clear out corruption, it seems relevant. The hope must be that sufficient democratic principle will remain to balance the inevitable money-making by politicians. The remark about money and power politics referred to in the newspaper account was a statement of Kishi's to the effect that politics is power, and power is money. It is a firmly rooted belief.

Okada saw his work as a race against time. Naturally he was optimistic and was obliged to paint as rosy a picture as possible. The Conservatives, he said, were acquiring greater strength through creeping bureaucracy:

"Kishi is a bureaucrat at heart. Even before the war he was a bureaucrat holding a cosy seat in Tojo's Cabinet. We must be powerful enough to check him. We must see that opposition doesn't dwindle. It is true that as a nation we love authority. We are like the Germans. Yet the newspapers are working on the right side, so that people believe both in authority and in democracy. Their minds are confused, but education will help them. Our strength has not yet been great enough to get proper education. There is no tradition of democracy. The Japanese still believe that government for the people is more important than government by the people. But over the Police Bill we won. Kishi tried to strengthen the police in order to return to the pre-war situation, but we defeated him."

Okada is an optimist and, to some extent, even he is a slave of his slogans. He believes things because they are said rather than because they are thought out. In his own field of foreign politics, he had an approach which was totally unreal and which was dictated by the precept of peace which the Japanese have all embraced but which the Socialist Party believes even more strongly. Okada could see no necessity for an alliance with the United States. His colleague, Asanuma, who had recently come back from China, issued a joint communiqué together with the Chinese to the effect that America was the common enemy of China and Japan. Okada had facile explanations for this rather unexpected statement, insisting that the Chinese draft of the communiqué would never have been shown to the Japanese because the Chinese delegation thought they would not accept it. He said that there was no need for any military pact with America for neither the Russians nor the Chinese would ever wish to occupy Japan. There was no need for any American bases, for in the event of war the Americans would abandon them and were only likely to use them as a base to attack from.

"We are not rich and we have not much food—there would be no purpose in occupying us."

I pointed out that Japan was in reality the most highly

developed country industrially in the whole of Asia. Surely he must see that anyone attacking America would have to occupy Japan.

"Ah well," he said, "we have nice girls. They would soon get the morale down of any occupying nation."

I began to wonder whether perhaps it wasn't just as well that he agreed that his party had no chance of coming into power for at least ten years.

Nakasone, the young Conservative member of the Diet who many people think will one day be Prime Minister, on the other hand, seemed to me to justify many of Okada's fears and also made me wonder whether the Socialists had any hope of winning the race. I lunched with him one day, soon after meeting Okada, and was once again surprised at the mental agility of the Japanese in managing to believe, or anyhow state, two totally contrary opinions.

He was a much smoother, sleeker figure than Okada, having none of the bonhomie of his opponent and all of the arrogance of the successful Japanese man. He gave me a long sales talk about his admiration for England and the English parliamentary system, for his great hope, he said, was of a bi-party democracy succeeding in Japan. But as soon as he had said it he told me that he did not really believe in an opposition. They were a splendid thing to have about, as long as there was no question of their gaining power. He certainly bore out Okada's opinion of the determination of the Conservatives to remain in power. The Constitution of Japan, he said, should be amended.

"We should have either a parliamentary cabinet system or a presidential system under the Emperor. The Prime Minister should be elected by the people or by Parliament. But we want stability, we do not want a constant seesaw of parties. Your Prime Minister is not stable. It is difficult if the Prime Minister is always in danger. He cannot promote a long-term policy. Policy cannot be by the direct will of the people."

He believed that education should be supervised by the government.

"But," he said, "we should never give direct orders carried out by force, nor should we show only one point of view or ideology, but we should teach citizenship."

The directive of the education ministry which I quoted at him states that from 1961 the singing of the national anthem *Kimigayo*, shall be compulsory in all music lessons—1959 and 1960 being set aside as a preparatory period. This has caused much trouble amongst the teachers' union, in company with a number of other rather more serious edicts. But I used it because it is regarded by some people as the beginnings of a restoration of emperor worship. Nakasone was not to be drawn on this.

"You would be surprised by what young people say about the Emperor. My children, for instance, say the Imperial family is an unwarranted tax expense."

Nakasone was to be drawn on very few points. When I talked to him about corruption he said, "Surely it is all right if you read about it in the newspapers?"

And when I suggested that eleven thousand people was a great many people to have to amnesty, he answered, "Don't you have amnesties in England for political violators?"

"We might have to," I said, "if we had so many of them."

All in all, they were an alarming pair, the one grappling for a power which I felt he would abuse as freely as the other one who was struggling to keep it.

These two men are nothing more than a surface manifestation of ill-adjustment. There is a deeper disease which stems from Japan's strange history.

It has occurred to me that the cutting off of Japan for two hundred and fifty years from all contact with the rest of the world was in a way something like a delicate child, unable to go to school, being educated at home by its mother. The child will learn some things. It may even become astonishingly proficient in one or two fields, but for the rest of its life it will be separate in some way from the ordinary world. This is what has happened to Japan. The quirks remain. But a nation lives longer than a man, and the adjustment must be attainable.

My account of the country, consisting as it does of incidents and pictures, gives at one level a false impression. It may explain what I saw, but it cannot take account of the difference which I referred to between human nature and human behavior. I have been concerned with the behavior, and hoped that nature would show through. The war crimes of the Japanese, which seems to be the thing which obsesses most of the people who ask me about Japan, are simply a question of behavior. The climate of prewar Japan is hard to recapture, but they were expected to be convinced that they were a race of divine origin. You might think that in a history written for tourists they would have hesitated to parade the more manifest absurdities of their beliefs. But writing in 1939 for the tourist library Koya Nakamura said:

"The relations between the Imperial family and the people today may therefore be likened to those between the trunk and branches of a gigantic tree. For if we were to trace the genealogy of each Japanese subject we should find that he belongs to a family which centuries ago was either a direct or indirect offshoot of the Imperial family."

The author claimed that everyone, whatever his name, belonged to one of four families, each descended from an emperor, and concluded that all Japanese were therefore descended from Amaterasu, the mythical sun goddess founder of the Imperial family.

The Japanese believed, quite genuinely, that they were a race apart. The hysteria of emperor worship cannot be exaggerated. Orders from an officer were orders from the Emperor. Therefore when the soldiers were ordered to butcher or torture prisoners they really had no feeling that they were dealing with other human beings. Stretching the point a little, it might be possible to compare their reactions to those of a people attacked by a race of super apes. But whatever the causes, they were causes dictated by a code of behavior carefully fostered by the military class. There is nothing in the nature of Japanese people which makes them crueller than any other people. They perpetrated nothing so calculatedly evil as the German Jewish atrocities. Their behavior was the product of two hundred and fifty years' isolation, an isolation which turned them in on themselves, perverting and twisting them so that certain facets of their culture became impossibly exaggerated.

In this sphere the cure has been effected; the need was imperative and the remedy drastic. The Americans, while perhaps overenthusiastic and comically naïve, with an eager faith in their own way of life, believing it to be applicable and even operable in any society, performed a remarkably difficult task far better than they are given credit for. The politicians' antics may be a strange interpretation of democracy as we believe in it, but there are among the young people those who now believe almost instinctively in the precepts which the Americans endeavored to instill. I consider this to be an amazing tribute to the mocked-at sincerity of the Americans. But, if democracy is to triumph, much more must be corrected than the caricature exaggerations which produced militarism and war crimes.

In other spheres the need for a remedy has not been so immediate. But until those other spheres are similarly purged there can be no hope of complete safety for the country. It isn't only a question of saying that if you take off your kimono you can walk more freely—it is a matter of digging out the dead tendrils of a rotted web of roots. It may seem a harsh prescription that a people should be asked to abandon all that they believe has made them great. But such greatness as they had was real only in a world so far removed from the needs of present reality as now to be farcical. The *kabuki* theater seems to me to symbolize much that is amiss with Japan. It is beautiful, certainly, and to foreigners it is intriguing as it would be to come across in Warwickshire an unknown little village where Shakespeare was still acted in the same way as in Elizabethan times. That is the exact parallel—the style, the movements, the words, the sentiments have remained unchanged. They do not pretend to bear any relation to modern life. It is quite some time since the female parts in Shakespeare were played by men, but the female parts in *kabuki* are still performed by male actors. *Kabuki* is an interesting art form, but it is in some ways a petrified one.

The Japanese films which are shown in foreign countries might seem to be a complete contradiction of this theory. But the average film has even less content than the average *kabuki* play. Certainly the good films are excellent and the men who make them representative of the few emancipated Japanese. Yet, even such a film as *Living*, perhaps one of the best, depends for much of its effect upon the conflicts of tradition with enterprise, emphasizing the strength of the past.

The Japanese still build their houses in precisely the same style they have been built for centuries. There are office blocks and official buildings erected in the twentieth-century Western manner, but any Japanese man of forty will tell you that he would prefer to retire to a house designed according to the patterns of his ancestors. It is as if every Englishman's ambition were to build himself a black-and-white half-timbered home; as if every American wished to retire to a log cabin.

The businessmen are still weighed down with the obligations of the old system of courtesy so that they cannot just pick up the telephone and order twelve gross of anything, but must pound out to a little teahouse and exchange the time of goodness knows how many days before a deal can be completed. Doctors will maintain the curious fiction that it is all their fault if even the most moribund of patients dies. The scene at a hospital is very odd; each member of the family will bow and thank the doctor, and the doctor will turn to each and say, "My skill was not great enough."

Much is touching, much is beautiful, nearly all is decorous. Why alter it, why force a change? The answer lies in the twelve million people who live below subsistence level. I remember one old weaver of about sixty, sitting before his loom passing the shuttle to and fro, his specially ridged finger-nails catching at threads, creating an exquisitely elaborate piece of brocade. He made an inch each day. For his employer he earned three thousand dollars a year; for himself he earned two hundred and eighty dollars.

It is not pretty to see the tired faces of the students and the housewives on the streetcars—faces which sink on to their chests in an apathetic sleep as soon as the car moves off. It is not pleasant to realize that a student may live and work in half a four-mat room, perched above another as if in a railroad sleeping car. It is not an agreeable sight to watch the children in winter with a livid sore patch beneath each nostril and to hear them cough with the beginnings of tuberculosis.

Plainly a love of tradition cannot alone be blamed for the misfortunes of Japan. More important by far is the fearful problem of overpopulation. In spite of amazing strides in birth control the population of the country is still rising at the rate of one million every year.

The land can yield little more. Industry is Japan's only chance of competing in a modern world. Here too the advances have been remarkable. So remarkable that she has left all other Asian countries far behind.

But, throughout my stay, I was reminded again and again of the words of the Emperor Chokei, writing rather feebly in the 1370's instead of doing something:

> 'Tis an age of disquiet
> Too full, alas, of strife to allow
> Of a day of cherry-blossom viewing

CHAPTER THIRTEEN

THE QUAYSIDE

WE left Japan by ship. There is somehow something much more final in the departure of a liner than in the taking off of an airplane. There is too much time in which to consider the actual fact of going. One has to be on board early and, instead of stepping straight into another world, one can as it were drag onto the ship some of the elements of the place which one is leaving. So it was with our going.

They all came on board, our Japanese friends, and for once it was in us that the tension was almost unbearable. There we were on familiar ground, in a British ship, still thinking in a Japanese fashion—almost disbelieving, almost resentful of the easy contact which one made with the seamen, with the stewards and with the other passengers.

As for our Japanese friends, they for once were almost liberated, quite surprisingly uncontorted; for grief at parting is an emotion which can freely be given rein. Obā San, who had sat on the temple veranda pouring out tea and had announced in between shrieks and giggles of laughter, "This is the day my son was killed"—and we all had to laugh with her—now wept. Osho San, incongruous yet enormously dignified in the main lounge of the boat, and, at the same time,

255

fascinated with a schoolboy enthusiasm by everything to do with the ship—it was another *hajimete* for him—intrigued by the fact that he could get so many American cigarettes merely by my signing for them, was strangely moved.

The students came in succession throughout the afternoon, all pledging their friendship:

"And you too, please always be my friend, and if I ever come to your country, please honor me by receiving me as your one-time Japanese companion."

The children's nurse and the cook, both suddenly tiny and almost cowering in the corridors, cried as I had never seen people in such a situation cry. And lastly Moku, in his hunting beret, arriving late and at a moment of inopportune confusion, yet managing with his boyish expertise to get aboard without a card long after everyone was meant to have left.

Finally the boat sailed, with that curious mixture of tragedy and ritual to which we had become so accustomed. From the top of the long customs shed a brass band played with unfair sentimentality.

From below on the dock, friends, relations, the whole mass of upturned faces, throwing up to those on the ship an endless flutter of paper streamers. It was again the same as Martha's departure from Shikoku, but now multiplied by twenty times the tearing apart.

The band beat out with pathetic idiocy "Auld Lang Syne" over and over again, while the dwindling figures clutched, until the last moment, the strands of colored paper with their forlorn symbolism. When the figures on the quay had become only indistinguishable faces crowned with black, identical hair, the last streamer broke and we were gone.